PRAISE FOR *LEADERSHIP ON THE ROCKS*

"Bethany Rees brilliantly captures the chaos and opportunity of leadership in *Leadership on the Rocks*. Her relatable analogies—like the Valley of Despair to the Mountaintop of Promotion—help leaders see themselves in the story, making it easier to take action. The Head, Heart, Hands, and Guts framework is both intuitive and empowering, offering real-world tools to thrive, not just survive. Bethany's honesty and practical wisdom make this a book every leader needs."

—Michele Smith, CEO of Better Possibilities

"Finally, a leadership book that combines practicality with purpose! Bethany Rees goes beyond the usual buzzwords and dives into the essence of effective leadership. The Leadership on the Rocks Framework has transformed the way I prioritize my time and energy. Instead of chasing the 'sand' in my work, I'm now building a foundation that aligns with universal principles and best practices. This survival kit is a game-changer!"

—Jamie Rayford, COO, Batesville Area Chamber of Commerce

"If you want harmony between your professional and personal life, read this book! *Leadership on the Rocks* will give you the right proactive tools to get ahead of the daily fires you are always fighting and to go home to your family with less stress."

—Christopher Povich, Ed.D., assistant superintendent for high schools

"Bethany Rees has hit a home run as she turns her personal leadership story into an impactful leadership guide. The Leadership on the Rocks Framework will give you the right proactive tools to get ahead of the daily fires that for too long have captured our focus as leaders. The eight resources in the survival kit are practical ways to prioritize time and energy. This guide is a game-changer for you and the leaders on your team!"

—John and Kelly Sherrill, lead and co-pastors of Declaration Church

LEADERSHIP ON THE ROCKS

HOW TO SURVIVE, ADAPT, AND SUCCEED IN THE WILDERNESS OF LEADERSHIP

BETHANY REES

LEADERSHIP ON THE ROCKS
How to Survive, Adapt, and Succeed in the Wilderness of Leadership

Copyright © 2025 by Bethany Rees

All rights reserved. No part of this book may be reproduced, distributed, or transmitted in any form or by any means, including photocopying, recording, or other electronic or mechanical methods, without the written permission from the publisher or author, except as permitted by U.S. copyright law or in the case of brief quotations embodied in a book review.

Disclaimer: This book has been published for the purpose of providing the reader with general information on its subject matter. The author and the publisher believe the information to be accurate and authoritative at the time of publication. The book is sold with the understanding that neither the author nor the publisher is providing professional advice, and the reader should not rely upon this book as such. Every situation is different, and professional advice (whether psychological, legal, financial, tax, or otherwise) should only be obtained from a professional licensed in your jurisdiction who has knowledge of the specific facts and circumstances.

Cover Design by Abigael Elliott
Interior Layout and Design by Alice Briggs
Editorial Team: Traci Matt, Chloie Benton, Cindy Venable

ISBNs:
Ebook: 979-8-89165-260-6
Paperback: 979-8-89165-261-3
Hardcover: 979-8-89165-268-2

Published by:
Streamline Books
Kansas City, MO
streamlinebookspublishing.com

DEDICATION

To my husband Jason —

For every leadership book we read, every podcast we dissected, and every car ride conversation where we turned leadership principles into plans for both work and home—Thank you for leading beside me, laughing with me, and loving me through every chapter of this journey.

CONTENTS

Praise for *Leadership on the Rocks* I
Dedication VII
Preface XI

Part 1: Becoming a Leader 1
   Chapter 1: Destination Leadership 3
   Chapter 2: The Leadership on the Rocks Survival Kit 13

Part 2: The Head of Leadership 19
   Chapter 3: Mindset 21
   Chapter 4: Identity 39
   Chapter 5: Purpose 57

Part 3: The Heart of Leadership 73
   Chapter 6: Relationships 75
   Chapter 7: Communication 91
   Chapter 8: Collaboration 111

Part 4: The Hands of Leadership 127
   Chapter 9: Execution 129
   Chapter 10: Systems and Processes 151
   Chapter 11: Service 167

Part 5: The Guts of Leadership......................181
    Chapter 12: Accountability........................183
    Chapter 13: Stewardship..........................199
    Chapter 14: Legacy...............................213
Epilogue: Thriving on the Rocks 227
Acknowledgements 229
Endnotes 233

PREFACE

THIS LEADERSHIP BOOK is unlike any other you've ever read. I present to you a survival kit loaded with tools to help you adapt and succeed in the wilderness of leadership. The framework in this guide would have launched my career faster and saved me from sleepless nights, stressful days, and anxiety-ridden conflicts. I created it to save you from the same fate.

Most leadership books talk about taking your leadership to the "next level" or focus on one concept. But what about leaders who are new or struggling at their current level and need all the concepts?

As the everyday leader who wrote this book, I have a personal leadership story that is one of struggle. I was a high-achieving individual contributor who was promoted into leadership, then struggled because I was unprepared for the sheer number of challenges I faced.

As my influence grew, so did my exposure to chaos, and I was unprepared for the reality of dealing with it. I felt as though I had crash-landed onto a battlefield with bombs of conflict going off, bullets of problems flying overhead, and hidden minefields of constraints everywhere.

My day-to-day life felt like a revolving door of negativity, stress, and overwhelming circumstances. I was constantly putting out fires to prevent them from burning my leadership house down.

It was these overwhelming situations that led me to say, "No more." I wanted to thrive professionally without sacrificing my family life. I had always been a student of leadership, but I didn't need more theory; I needed a practical guide to navigate my way out of the chaotic wilderness I felt trapped in. So I built a framework I could live and lead by.

With every problem, conflict, and constraint I faced, I took notes on things I wished I had known and would have done differently. I collected theories and turned them into real-life applications. The result of all my hard lessons is this survival kit—everything I wish I'd had access to early in my leadership career.

Leaders, you can have harmony in and between your work and family lives. I've experienced this transformation myself. The behaviors and skills I've learned through this framework have made me not just a better and more successful leader but a better spouse and parent.

Being in a leadership position shouldn't ruin your life with overwhelming stress. It should be an opportunity for you to excel professionally, personally, and financially.

Through this survival guide, you'll become equipped with the tools, skills, and behaviors to not only survive but thrive in leadership. You'll learn to confidently make a positive impact without sacrificing your home life in the process. You'll discover how to transform from being a manager of the status quo to being a leader of impact.

PREFACE

Thank you for joining me on this journey. May it be a transformative one.

As a thank you for investing in this book, I want to give you a free Leadership on the Rocks workbook to help you apply the lessons to your specific work situation. Download your free workbook by going to www.leadershipontherocks.com/freeworkbook.

PART 1
Becoming a Leader

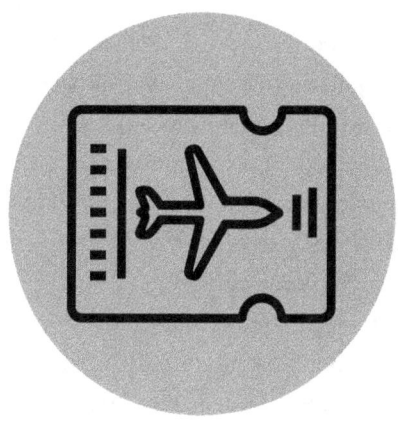

CHAPTER 1

Destination Leadership

IT'S NOT SUPPOSED to feel this way. A promotion, I mean. Most of us like the thought of a promotion. Getting the invitation to step into a leadership position sounds like a dream. The epitome of what we work toward in our career is to one day have a fancy title, a big paycheck, and the power to illuminate our expertise.

Yes, becoming a leader, or a person of influence, is a goal most of us hope to achieve at some point in our lives.

I know I did. But that excitement only lasted a few weeks until reality set in and my leadership "high" quickly came crashing down.

I began my leadership career as a teacher leading a classroom of thirty kids. From there it evolved into leading teams of teachers. Eventually, I earned a skip-level promotion to become a high school administrator for a brand-new 6A high school in Texas.

Stepping into that administrative role for the first time, I was so excited to be able to make an even greater impact on children's lives, teachers' work environment, and the community as a whole. But as I said, that excitement dwindled rapidly as it hit me that I was in charge of hundreds of employees and responsible for thousands of students, all while starting an organization from scratch. Those were the hardest years of my leadership life.

When I began this leadership role, all I heard was, "Congratulations on the promotion," and "Reach out to others if you need anything." Need anything? I felt like I needed *everything*: onboarding, clarity of job expectations, a mentor, and more.

As with most job descriptions, mine only listed the tip of the iceberg of the full requirements. I quickly became overwhelmed by the many demands for my time and attention. Each day required me to put out what seemed like never-ending fires in a multitude of areas.

The anxiety and stress I felt from the chaos took its toll on my physical health and family life. I began working longer hours to get it all done. I stayed awake at night thinking of all the things I hadn't finished that day, and my ability to be truly present with my family faded. As my husband would say, "I was a hot mess."

In talking with other leaders, especially new leaders, I've heard many say they had the same experience—crash-landing into leadership and becoming shocked and almost traumatized by the chaos of it.

Most of these people were amazing individual contributors and could really get the work done before they became leaders. Their yearly evaluations were full of praise but very little feedback about areas of improvement. They got used to receiving affirmation and validation for a job well done. They were such high-performing employees that they eventually got offered a promotion for the role of manager, supervisor, administrator, director, leader, or any number of shepherding roles.

But here's the truth for those who have received a stamped ticket to their dream promotion: They typically find that the experience is completely and utterly nothing like they imagined. In fact, the experience is so far from what they expected that many try to find ways to run away from the once-desired destination.

Let's take a closer look at what this journey into leadership really feels like for a new leader.

The Mountaintop of Promotion

Hooray! Congratulations to our new manager who got a stamped ticket to enter the land of leadership.

This destination has always looked exciting to her because from a distance, those in the land of leadership have the power and authority to make real change happen. Not only that, they have the improved paycheck that allows them to drive better cars, plan better vacations, and take better care of their employees.

The perception from afar is that on the other side of leadership, life is better.

And so our new manager is boarding the plane of promotion, beyond excited about her new position. She does, after all, have big dreams about all the things she's going to accomplish since she's no longer "just an employee."

Her thoughts start to run wild with ideas of how to make the product or service better, how to help the team grow, and how to help the organization become the best it can be. As the ideas for positive change are flowing in our new leader's head, so are the endorphins from the achievement of receiving the advancement.

As her excitement and anticipation about her first day in the land of leadership grows, she can see herself stepping off the plane of promotion and into the experience of a lifetime as a leader. As she gets closer to her arrival, her passion for positive change builds, as do her expectations for how everything is going to play out.

She can see it all in her head—gliding gracefully down the airstairs with a crowd of employees and other leaders welcoming her into leadership land. She envisions a leader concierge arriving at her side, ready to give her the grand tour.

She anticipates the employees sharing the fruit of their labor and asking her for fresh ideas. She expects to continue doing what she's always done—achieving success by getting desired results—and she hopes that all the positive change she brings to the land will be applauded and celebrated.

But that's not what happens. Not at all.

The Landslide of Reality

For our new manager, the landing from the plane of promotion to leadership land is anything but smooth.

Instead, just before descent, her supervisor gives her a handbook—it's a rudimentary parachute at best—and says, "Welcome to your new role," before nonchalantly throwing her from the plane.

Within a matter of moments, her excitement turns into sheer terror as she begins falling hard and fast toward a small mountainous island. With a thud she crashes onto the new terrain she would soon come to know as her new leadership role.

In shock, our new leader finds herself stranded on the rocks of an unknown landscape with no means for survival.

She quickly becomes disoriented, not knowing which way she is supposed to go. There is no survival kit to support her and no map in her handbook to provide guidance for how to navigate her unknown rocky terrain.

Brushing off her bruised ego, she thinks back to her college days and some leadership paths she learned. She chooses a direction and begins walking. With no clue as to whether the direction she is walking is right, wrong, or neutral, she continues forward until she encounters a few locals.

The natives smile and begin speaking to the new leader as though to welcome her to their mountainous home, but the greetings are in a dialect she's not familiar with. The locals' constant use of team jargon and acronyms confuses her.

While at first appearing friendly, the locals quickly turn hostile as they point to the sky and shout with anger. In doing her best to interpret the messages from the group, she gleans that they are discontent because the plane in the sky keeps dropping new leaders and mandates from above.

She continues to walk with the group, trying to interpret their story, when another band of locals greets them with suspicion and distrust. A conflict quickly breaks out as both groups begin pointing fingers as if to blame each other for the tribe's problems.

As she stands listening, trying to understand both sides, she struggles to see the whole picture due to a lack of common language and the backstory of the issues. So she takes her best guess at the root cause of the conflict and gathers that the tribe and its alpine habitat are experiencing extensive problems—problems our leader was completely unaware of before accepting the position.

In doing her best to mediate the growing interpersonal conflict, she is unable to see what is lurking just around the bend. She and the locals are blindly walking into what will feel like Jumanji Level 5—constraints.

With one false step, our leader is the first to fall into this booby trap of constraints and become trapped in the landslide of reality. The landslide begins to pick up speed, giving her even more problems, conflicts, and constraints than are humanly possible to escape.

With all the negativity suffocating her as she slides down the rugged landscape, she begins reaching out to grasp anything that could help her move to safety or at least allow her to catch her breath. But the gravitational pull is too great, and down our new leader goes.

The Valley of Despair

The rushing landslide finally slows its momentum, and our new manager finds herself lying at the base of the mountainous landscape, landing once again on the rocks. As she climbs out of the crisis she just experienced, she finds herself out of breath, battered, and bruised. She's in a state of shock and still surrounded by chaos. All the problems, conflicts, and constraints came right down the mountain with her.

As her first week on the job turns into her first month, her first quarter, and her first year, not much changes. Every day is filled with restless locals, major problems, more conflict, and those never-ending restrictions on much-needed resources.

Her idealism about how her first year in leadership would go built expectations that were a far cry from the "on the rocks" reality she's experiencing. She had such big goals for implementing positive change, but due to the continuing daily chaos, she goes to bed every night feeling like a failure.

Feeling stuck in the valley of despair, she can't see how things could ever get better. As fatigue and a sense of failure wear her down, our leader inevitably gives in to the status quo. She no longer has a desire to inspire positive change but begins accepting things as they are.

Influenced by her own cynicism, she now believes that things will never change. She has lost hope and sees her leadership as forever "on the rocks." For her, "on the rocks" has become synonymous with instability, failure, and despair—a place where leaders crash and burn, unable to recover.

Escaping the Valley and Conquering the Rocks

If our leader's story feels painfully similar to your own journey into leadership, just know that you are not alone. Sadly, it's an all too common experience.

But what if being "on the rocks" didn't refer to the struggle of leadership? What if, instead of a place of failure, it could become a foundation for strength?

The truth is that rocks are some of the most stable and enduring structures in nature. They withstand pressure, hold firm under weight, and offer footing when the ground beneath us feels unsteady. Leadership "on the rocks" doesn't have to mean brokenness; it can mean resilience, stability, and security.

Iconic author and thought leader Stephen Covey epitomized the importance of rocks in a beautiful analogy in his book *The 7 Habits of Highly Effective People.*[1] He says that effective people put first things (rocks) first.

Thus, rocks represent focusing on our priorities.

Long before Stephen Covey used the analogy of big rocks, Jesus used a parable about rocks as a call to apply the moral and ethical living taught in his Sermon on the Mount.

> Everyone then who hears these words of mine and does them will be like a wise man who built his house *on the rock*. And the rain fell, and the floods came, and the winds blew and beat on that house, but it did not fall, because it had been founded *on the rock*. And everyone who hears these words of mine and does not do them will be like a foolish man who built his house on the sand. And the rain fell, and the floods came, and the winds blew and beat against that house, and it fell, and great was the fall of it (Matthew 7:24–27, emphasis added).

Thus, rocks characterize a stable foundation that can withstand any storm it encounters.

We can intentionally transform the experience of having a job on the rocks that makes us want to have a drink on the rocks by redefining the phrase into a powerful reminder that no matter how rocky the terrain, leaders can find their footing, steady themselves, and build something lasting.

Whether you've been stuck in the rugged valley of despair for just a couple of months or for more years than you can count, you don't have to stay there! As of this moment, you can start climbing out and up one step at a time so you can better navigate any rocky landscape you encounter.

The key lies in packing and using the Leadership on the Rocks survival kit—a tool kit of essential resources and strategies to help you not just survive the challenges of leadership but thrive because of them. These tools will empower you to climb higher, build stronger, and lead with resilience, even in the face of life's toughest terrain.

CHAPTER 2

The Leadership on the Rocks Survival Kit

MY PERSONAL LEADERSHIP story is one of struggle. As a high-achieving individual contributor who was promoted into leadership, I packed for my destination in expectation of traveling to paradise. But the experience I encountered was that of being dropped in an unknown rocky mountain range without the tools to sustain survival.

> Leadership is not a destination to be achieved. Leadership is a body to be nourished and protected.

As my leadership influence grew, so did my exposure to the harsh and unforgiving elements of the landscape around me. I felt as though I had crash-landed "on the rocks" where jagged edges of conflict cut deep, unstable boulders of problems shifted underfoot, and slippery gravel of constraints threatened to pull me off balance at every step.

What I quickly learned from my days of chaos was this: Leadership is not a destination to be achieved. Leadership is a body to be nourished and protected.

The Body of Leadership

If you were to really land on a mountain of rocks with unforgiving terrain all around, you wouldn't fret over how you looked or what other people thought about you. Rather, you'd be completely focused on your most basic needs: nourishment (water and food), protection (shelter and clothing), and then a plan for thriving in your new environment.

Most human beings know their basic needs to survive a physically challenging situation, but in our metaphorical scenario, new or struggling leaders don't always know their basic needs and the tools needed to survive any type of leadership situation. Instead they get caught up in unessential and nonurgent tasks like checking their email or attending every meeting they have been invited to.

Just as your physical body needs nourishment and protection to survive, so does your leadership body. If cared for appropriately, the body of leadership will be able to not only withstand immense amounts of pressure (conflicts and problems), but thrive despite any parching environment (constraints) it may find itself in.

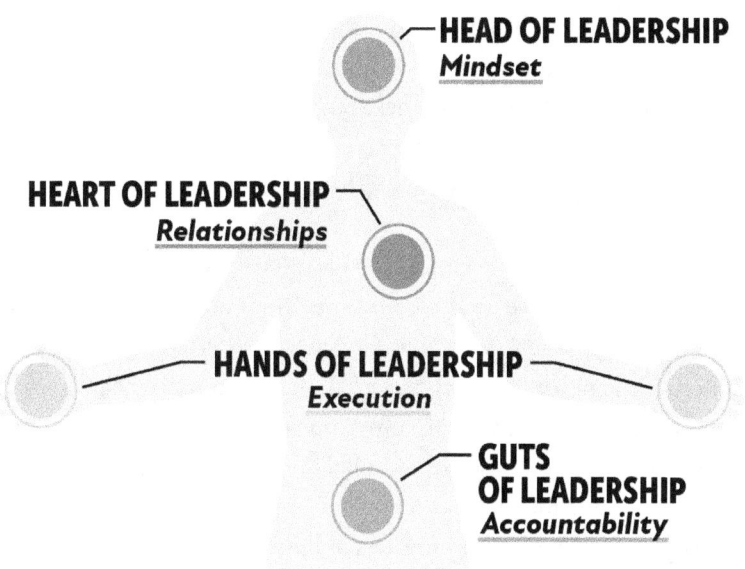

The head, heart, hands, and guts of leadership are the four critical areas of leadership you must focus on nourishing and protecting. In every situation as a leader, you will need to utilize leadership thinking, relationship influence, results-driven execution, and accountability for growth and progress.

These four areas not only sustain your life in leadership, but they also add stability and longevity to the "body" of your work. If you nourish and protect these four areas with the most essential resources, you are not only going to survive, but you are going to be thriving in your leadership. However, if these four areas are ignored, malnourished, or threatened, what will ensue is chaos, stress, and hopelessness.

The Eight Essential Survival Resources

My family and I absolutely love going on new adventures. From exploring small-town festivals to hiking in state and national parks, we are always looking for our next outdoor experience. However, in preparing for these new encounters in unknown territories, I take great pride in proclaiming myself the ultimate packer of the family backpack.

My goal with our backpack is to ensure we always have the most essential resources we need for our expeditions no matter the terrain, weather, or situation we may find ourselves in. Not only do I focus on our basic needs (water and snacks), but I'm sure to include other tools to support a fun and safe adventure (trail/festival info, cash, wet wipes, ponchos, multiuse pocketknife, first aid kit, portable chargers, and a deck of cards).

As people grow in their positions of influence, it is imperative that they too pack their own backpack of vital supplies that will nourish and protect their body of leadership and ensure a positive experience.

While there are a lot of leadership tools available, the Leadership on the Rocks survival kit provides leaders with the eight most important resources to strengthen and safeguard them in any "on the rocks" circumstance they might encounter so that the overall experience will be worthwhile.

The essential resources (or universal principles) within the four critical areas of the leadership body serve as the provisions for your overall health, wellness, and abundance.

THE LEADERSHIP ON THE ROCKS SURVIVAL KIT

THE LEADERSHIP ON THE ROCKS FRAMEWORK

THE BODY OF LEADERSHIP	THE EIGHT ESSENTIAL RESOURCES	
HEAD OF LEADERSHIP *Mindset*	 IDENTITY	 PURPOSE
HEART OF LEADERSHIP *Relationships*	 COMMUNICATION	COLLABORATION
HANDS OF LEADERSHIP *Execution*	 SYSTEMS & PROCESSES	 SERVICE
GUTS OF LEADERSHIP *Accountability*	 STEWARDSHIP	 LEGACY

Each tool is a sustainable resource designed to nourish and protect the body of leadership: the head, heart, hands, and guts. When leaders pack and utilize these supplies, they discover strategies for mindset, relationships, execution, and accountability that ensure their survival and success.

With the Leadership on the Rocks survival kit, every person of influence will have the tools to not only find their footing (survive) but build an unshakeable foundation that strengthens and sustains their leadership legacy (thrive).

By ensuring you always have these eight resources, your leadership body will always have the provisions it needs to withstand any terrain or climate you find yourself in. Not only do these tools anchor your thoughts, beliefs, feelings, and behaviors to leadership principles, but they will also help you navigate and flourish in any environment whether at work or home.

Be mindful to care for your body of leadership by providing it what it needs to survive and thrive in any situation. Nourishing and strengthening your body of leadership, or the lack thereof, doesn't just affect you. It impacts everyone around you. Taking time to fill your leadership survival kit with these vital essentials isn't "a nice thing to do"; it's demanded of you if you want to make a positive impact.

PART 2
The Head of Leadership

Navigating Your Leadership Role

CHAPTER 3

Mindset

The GPS Command Center

ONE TIME, AS my family and I were hiking around Pinnacle Mountain State Park in central Arkansas, we got so caught up in seeing the sights and chatting that we stopped paying attention to trail signs. As our path became more arduous and unstable, we quickly became confused about which trail we were on and which direction we were supposed to go.

What should have been a short leisurely stroll that day turned into a long obstacle course that took hours to complete. We finally climbed high enough to get a cell phone signal to check our GPS trails app and identify the appropriate path back. From that moment on, our eyes were wide open looking for trail signs to stay on a secure path until we made it safely back to our car.

There is nothing that fills our lungs more than the fresh air found while hiking in the great outdoors. However, as I found out on that hiking adventure, there's nothing that will fill a person with anxiety and stress more than trying to navigate unknown and unstable ground.

But unlike hikers on a manicured state park trail, many employees are left to navigate the wilderness of their position and its terrain without posted signs and a clear path. Thus, it's imperative that we learn how to navigate our way through any landscape. Without knowing how to determine our location and get directions, the feeling of being lost can quickly escalate. We may move from a loss of our mental footing to the slippery slopes of anxiety and stress or worse, to panic and hysteria. Working out of any of these negative emotional states creates adverse consequences no one wants to fall into.

When it comes to nourishing and protecting the head of leadership, our mindset is our GPS command software to help us acclimate to and navigate within our new environment while hopefully avoiding its hazards.

What Is Mindset?

According to psychologist Gary Klein, "a mindset is a belief that orients the way we handle situations—the way we sort out what is going on and what we should do."[2]

Stanford University psychologist Carol S. Dweck goes even further to say that our lives are heavily influenced by our mindsets or how we think about our talents and abilities. She coined the mindset terms of *growth* (focused on learning skills) and *fixed* (focused on talent).[3] Stephen R. Covey coined the mindset terms for *abundance* (the belief more can always be created) and *scarcity* (the belief a finite amount exists).[4]

The Survival Connection

Navigating leadership is much like finding your way through the wilderness. Just as a hiker relies on a GPS tool to avoid getting lost by following secured routes, leaders depend on their mindset to guide them through challenges. The mindset we operate out of can act as either trail signs that keep us on the right path or distractions that entice us into the lurking dangers of selfishness, doubt, and negativity. Without the ability to recalibrate and refocus, we risk wandering aimlessly on insecure ground, expending energy but making no meaningful progress.

Imagine a hiker without a map, second-guessing every turn and constantly stumbling on loose rocks. Their growing frustration and fear can cloud judgment and lead to panic. Similarly, unchecked thoughts—fueled by assumptions, insecurities, or fears—can sidetrack leaders, pulling them away from their goals and into the slippery slope of "what ifs."

To lead effectively, we must shine a light on the stories, lies, and false narratives that clutter our thinking. Exposing these mental obstacles allows us to replace them with truths that nourish our confidence and clarity, enabling us to forge ahead with purpose.

The biggest battle you'll ever face in leadership, and in life, is the one in your own head. The head of leadership functions as our mental command center, much like a survivalist's navigation tools. It's where every decision, reaction, and plan originates.

Key Takeaway:

Your mindset, or how you think about things, affects your experiences.

If the head is clouded by confusion, stress, or a negative mindset, the leader becomes no better than a hiker lost in a tangled jungle without a compass. Leaders must learn to adjust their mindset settings, much like adjusting the settings on a GPS tool, to ensure they receive clear, accurate directions that keep them moving on a secure path toward their ultimate goal.

Thoughts, Emotions, and Actions: It's All Connected

Leadership is rarely a smooth, paved trail with clearly marked signs. It's more like a primitive, unmarked domain that demands creative problem-solving, adaptability, and persistence to navigate.

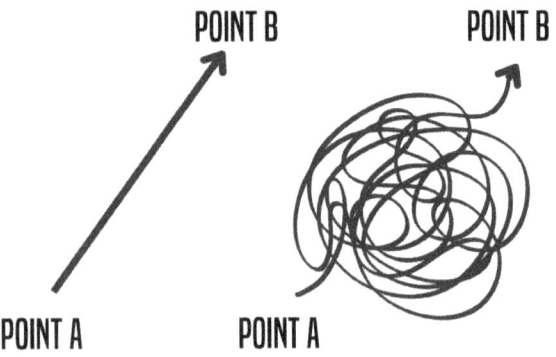

A mindset equipped for living in the jumbled reality can transform the wilderness of leadership into an opportunity to explore, grow, and achieve great things even when the terrain is rugged.

Our thoughts are the software controlling our internal GPS. They decode our environment and shape how we move forward by influencing our feelings, beliefs, behaviors, habits, and culture.

Your thoughts create your emotions, and your emotions drive your actions.

Thoughts → Emotions → Actions

In other words, it's not what happens externally that has you and me feeling stressed; it's what is happening internally. It's how we think about the gap between our expectations and the reality we live out that produces our anxiety and stress. If we want to not only survive leadership but thrive in it, then we need to know how to upgrade our GPS software so we can better navigate the internal mental wilderness we don't often realize we're wandering in.

Michelle Spadafora, health guru and founder of Faithful Workouts, puts it this way: "The workplace is full of circumstances and situations. It's our interpretation of those that can cause stress or not."[5]

Situations are just situations until we apply meaning to them with our internal feelings that then create our external reactions or responses. Through personal development, we can train our mind to better navigate the stimuli to win the battle of our thoughts and reduce our levels of stress.

Thus, if we want to not only survive but thrive in leadership, our journey has to start with analyzing what is going on in our thought life and where our first thoughts come from so we can learn to adjust them.

Mindset Adoption and Adjustment

Our mindsets are usually built from the views or beliefs about ourselves that we adopt based on our past experiences. It's here that we can become stuck in how we think about ourselves and the world around us.

Let's make this concrete with a short exercise. Take a moment to reflect on a few difficult experiences from your past and your interpretations of them.

What negative stories or labels did you hear or receive from others?
What negative stories or labels did you tell or give yourself?

> **Stories we hear from others:**
> "You'll never _____."
> "You're just a (insult) from (location)."
> "Without the _____, you're nothing."
> "You're such a _____."

> **Stories we tell ourselves:**
> "I can't do (or I'm just not good at) _____."
> "I don't have a _____ problem."
> "That's just the way _____ is."
> "I'm always _____."

How did those stories and labels shape your thoughts, emotions, and behaviors over time? Did they push you toward a fixed and/or scarcity mindset? Why?

Our mindsets are developed from the stories and labels we adopt from past experiences. They then act like the screen of our internal GPS, interpreting the world around us and displaying a version of reality for us to follow. Over time, the way our GPS processes and presents the map—accurate or not—becomes the mindset-projected reality we navigate, shaping how we see ourselves and others.

If we want to free ourselves from stress and despair, we have to learn how to change the projection. We have to first recognize how quickly we tell ourselves a story that aligns with our adopted mindset (confirmed bias) and react with emotions based upon that mindset. Once we become aware of this pattern, we can start rewriting the stories we tell ourselves and shift toward a healthier growth or abundance mindset.

If that exercise felt like a bit of a downer, not to worry. Here's the beautiful thing about mindsets—they can be recalibrated. Just as you can customize preferences on your GPS—choosing different routes, avoiding tolls, or switching from a 2D to 3D view—you can learn to fine-tune how you process and evaluate thoughts and feelings about people, experiences, or circumstances. It's simply a matter of discovering how to adjust those settings.

Before we get into how to do this, it'll be helpful to know your starting point. While you may exhibit a mix of all the mindsets, which mindset do you believe you default to the most, especially at work?

- Fixed
- Growth
- Scarcity
- Abundance

Developing a Leader Mindset

As a person of influence you will experience a lot of internal and interpersonal challenges. New supervisors especially feel bombarded with massive amounts of negative stimuli they never encountered as individual contributors.

Issues, friction, and limitations are a guarantee in leadership. The higher you are promoted, the more they increase and the bigger the dollar signs attached to them.

No matter the situation, you want to take leader-like actions to solve problems, resolve conflicts, and conquer constraints, but you can't change your emotions or actions without changing your thinking.

This is why you need to start with the mindset of a leader. To truly grow into a better leader, spouse, parent, family member, or friend, you have to pull back the curtains on how you engage with the world. By better understanding how your mind is naturally set to think about things, you can better learn how to adjust those settings to experience situations differently.

Developing a leader mindset will help you overcome the many internal and interpersonal challenges you will face. Without a healthy thought life, your emotions can go unchecked causing you to have disproportionate or inappropriate reactions to situations. Unhealthy internal messaging also correlates to higher stress levels and lower quality of life.

A leader mindset is not only a mix of the growth and abundance mindsets; there's another important component. A leader mindset also requires emotional intelligence (EI). Psychologist Daniel Goleman popularized this term in his book *Emotional Intelligence: Why It Can Matter More Than IQ* and identifies it as key for outstanding leadership.[6]

EI is simply the ability to identify and manage your own emotions (i.e., to be self-aware) as well as recognize and respond to the emotions of those around you (i.e., to be others aware). EI can help you to

- quickly recognize your emotions and what triggered them,
- identify your thinking habits and patterns,
- capture the stories you tell yourself,
- adjust your thinking (and therefore your emotions) in the moment, and
- become aware of and respond appropriately to the emotions of others.

Having a leader mindset (growth/abundance mindsets + emotional intelligence) gives you the skills you need to identify and adjust your thoughts, emotions, and actions (your internal GPS) in the moment so you can respond to the situation instead of reacting to it.

It's like having the power to put a situation in slow motion so you don't react out of the ruts (habits) of your thoughts. Instead, you have the time and capacity to choose the appropriate GPS settings to route a course to the most appropriate response for the situation at hand.

You may be asking, "Okay, but how do I develop a leader mindset?" There are four steps.

Step 1. Stop your natural flow of thoughts.

A crucial part of developing a leader mindset is learning to talk to yourself instead of listening to yourself.

When you listen to yourself, your natural thoughts (along with your emotions and reactions) are in control of you instead of the other way around, and they can spiral down quickly.

Talking to yourself, on the other hand, means slowing down the natural flow of your thoughts before they have a chance to spiral out of control. This can be as simple as saying something in your mind or even out loud that interrupts your go-to thought process.

My natural bent for thinking is perfectionism and people-pleasing, so learning to stop my natural flow of thoughts has been crucial to calm my stress as a leader. When I struggle with fixed or scarcity thoughts, I find it helpful to lean on my faith by quoting 2 Corinthians 10:5: "We destroy arguments and every lofty opinion raised against the knowledge of God, and *take every thought captive* to obey Christ" (emphasis added).

From this, I've developed a few mantras, or repeated slogans, that I recite to interrupt my natural thinking patterns: "Capture that thought." "Don't tell yourself a story." "Slow your roll." I find that when I fail to use my mantras, it's much easier for the fixed or scarcity thoughts to run their course internally, causing unhealthy emotions and unhelpful reactions.

When we allow a fixed or scarcity mindset to rule our thinking, it usually leads to big emotions and a threat-stress reaction (think fight or flight).

I've not only had overreactions myself but have seen this play out in other leaders too.

For example, early in my leadership career, I was facilitating a data conversation with our school faculty, and our principal didn't like some of the teacher's viewpoints on what the data was showing. He became argumentative and defensive.

At one point, he lost his cool. He stood up, yelled at us in frustration, then stomped out of the meeting, slamming the door behind him. It was almost impossible for our staff to pick up the shattered pieces of our work culture because his tantrum undermined any hopes of respect for him.

Looking at this situation backwards, his external actions were anything but leaderlike, and his emotions were plainly visible to everyone. He could have avoided this dramatic scene and its cultural repercussions had he built a leader mindset and known how to stop and capture his thoughts.

I want you to develop the skills to avoid these kinds of destructive behaviors by learning how to stop your natural tendencies of thinking and instead, talk to yourself in the moment. After all, it can take years to build a great leadership reputation but only a few seconds to destroy it.

2. Use Emotional Intelligence (EI) to reflect.

Once you've managed to stop your thoughts, the next step is to pause and observe what's going on emotionally—both internally and externally. This is where emotional intelligence (EI) comes into play. EI will help you better recognize what's really behind your feelings and the feelings of others. By becoming more self-aware and others aware, you'll be able to understand what's at stake within the situation.

My "go-to move" to help me use EI to reflect on the thoughts and feelings of myself and others is to ask questions such as these:

- What emotions am I feeling right now? Why?
- What are the emotions of others in the room? How do I know?
- What are likely to be the root causes of these emotions?

Sometimes it's difficult to answer these questions while still leading a meeting or engaging with a person or group. If this is the case, try calling for a five-minute break so you can run through these questions, and everyone can come back to the room with a fresh perspective.

It's important to note that this growth step only really works *after* you've stopped and captured your thoughts. You can't easily pause to reflect on your emotions and those of others if your thoughts are already on a slippery slope.

3. Reframe your perspective.

We've established that as our thoughts go, so goes everything else. Stopping your thoughts (step 1) and then growing your EI by reflecting on your emotions and those of people around you (step 2) prepare you for step 3: reframing.

As a leader stepping into the tidal wave of issues, you can internalize all of the stimuli and lose control of your thoughts, emotions, and behavior, or you can anchor yourself in the growth/abundance mindsets, enhanced by emotional intelligence, and see the bigger picture. How can you adjust your thinking in the moment and shift to a perspective that will lead to an appropriate response for the issue at hand?

I describe this as the act of reframing. Reframing your thoughts is choosing to look at things from a different perspective. You can reframe in multiple ways—through the GPS screen settings of truth, empathy, curiosity, gratitude, and other positive attributes—but the goal is to make your thoughts work in better service for all parties involved.

I personally find it helpful to reframe my thoughts with curiosity by asking questions like these:

- Am I assuming positive intent before jumping to negative conclusions?
- How can I zoom out to see the bigger picture?
- What can I control? What can I *not* control?

- How did I contribute to this problem? How can I contribute to fixing it?
- What is the lesson I can learn from this?

Questions like these encourage me to inquire more about the situation and ultimately see it from multiple perspectives. Reframing works best once I've already stopped any destructive thought patterns and observed my emotions and the emotions of others. Only then can I be truly free to be curious.

4. Choose.

After step 3, you are well equipped to handle challenging situations better than you did before. But now you have to make your move. You have to act. None of this stopping, reflecting, or reframing will mean much if you don't use it to inform your chosen actions. Developing a leader mindset includes learning to put it into practice.

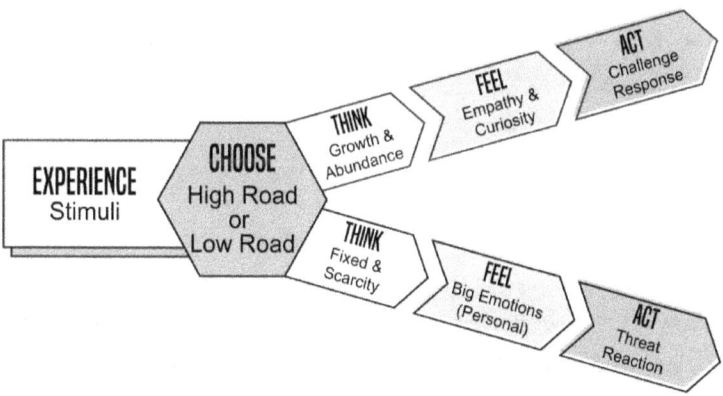

Your actions can take one of two paths—reaction or response. I like to think of reacting as the "low road" and responding as the "high road." The low road of leadership is a path born from reacting to stimuli (stressors) as threats; this reaction sends you into a fight-or-flight state (e.g., the leader in the example in step 1).

The high road, on the other hand, is a path born from responding to stimuli (stressors) as challenges; this response allows you to address issues calmly. This path is the natural continuation of following steps 1 through 3.

For a leader, the preference is clear. The high road means operating from a growth/abundance mindset and using emotional intelligence to address the issue at hand. The issue then feels like a challenge to overcome—an opportunity to solve a problem, resolve a conflict, or mitigate a constraint.

When you take the low road, you operate from a fixed/scarcity mindset that leads you to big emotions because you took things personally; you then react like you're under attack. This means you'll either escalate the issue or won't address it at all. Fighting or running away are not qualities of a great leader.

The leaders who don't know how to "slow their roll" and choose the high road are the ones who

- drive everyone crazy with their timidity or big emotions and overreactions,
- are closed-minded and hard to work with,
- are high-strung (e.g., sensitive, overwhelmed, anxious), and
- lose the respect and trust of the team.

Let me guess—someone specific just popped into your mind.

How do I know? Because those kinds of people exist in every organization. And while you can't change these leaders, you can certainly make sure you aren't one of them!

Those in leadership positions who can't capture their thoughts, use EI to reflect on their emotions, and reframe their perspectives to choose an appropriate response will always lose. They'll lose peace of mind. They'll lose valuable employees. They'll lose profits.

But the good news is that the opposite is also true: those in leadership who can (and do) capture their thoughts, use EI to reflect on their emotions, and reframe their perspectives to choose an appropriate response have healthier mental and physical boundaries on the job.

So the next time you find yourself in the middle of a fight-or-flight reaction, pause and reflect backward. How are you behaving? What have you said or done? How did your feelings prompt those behaviors? What thoughts created those feelings? Putting all of that together, what type of mindset sent you down the wrong path?

The more often you do this kind of reflection, the better you'll come to understand how you typically respond to challenges, disagreements, feedback, and competition. Once you understand your go-to responses and the thoughts and emotions that drive them, you can begin developing tools (e.g., mantras, reflection questions) that steer you away from the low road and keep you walking the high road.

Washing Off the Workday

If you don't learn to adjust your internal GPS settings to that of a leader mindset you'll not only get lost at work; you'll be disoriented at home too.

Your stress at work carries over into your home life.

But no matter how good you get at walking the high road, you'll still kick up dust, dirt, and debris that will cling to you. Dirt from a high road still makes you dirty.

Because of this, a leadership mindset also requires washing off that dirt at the end of the workday so you don't track it into your home. And I know a thing or two about dirt.

Let me explain.

One of the reasons I love exploring the outdoors is probably because I was raised on a farm in small-town Arkansas with dogs, chickens, pigs, cattle, and other random animals. While farm life taught me a strong work ethic, it also taught me to take off my work boots before entering the house. There is nothing more disgusting than walking around in your home barefoot only to step in dirt, mud, or worse. Ugh!

Just like you should take off your work boots so you don't make a mess in your house, you also need to learn how to "wash off" your workday before coming home. Do this so you don't track the mental and emotional muck from work around your house for you and your family to step in.

A wash-off-the-workday routine looks a bit different for each person, but the goal is to clear your mind and leave behind any stress before going home. For me, this includes doing a "brain dump" where I jot down everything floating around in my head. This helps me to close the thought loops and leave them on the paper (or screen) where I can find them the next day. My brain dump usually looks like a jumbled list of random and unprioritized tasks I need to complete: finish that report, schedule that meeting, call back that person, set up that training, check in on that person, set timers to walk this hallway, etc.

Then I like to listen to great music on my drive home. This helps me detach from any emotional tension or stress. I also pray during my commute so I can leave all my leadership thoughts and situations at the feet of God in exchange for receiving his peace and joy as I enter the door of my house. Then I put my phone away. I've learned that I don't have to be available 24/7 for texts and emails.

As you're working to develop a leader mindset, be sure you include a wash-off-the-workday routine. Family and friends shouldn't have to bear the weight of your leadership responsibilities when you step through the door.

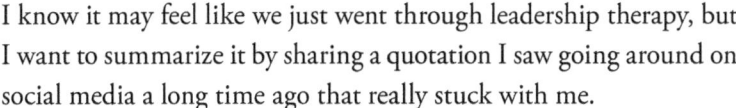

I know it may feel like we just went through leadership therapy, but I want to summarize it by sharing a quotation I saw going around on social media a long time ago that really stuck with me.

"When you finally learn that a person's behavior has more to do with their internal struggle than it ever did with you, you learn grace."[7]

I believe this is true. A lot is happening behind the scenes in the mind, and every human being has internal struggles that we know nothing about. This includes not only customers, stakeholders, and coworkers but also people in leadership positions.

Challenges and conflict will always come in leadership and life. We will have challenges in our day-to-day work and challenges in our marriages, parenting, careers, and social interactions. That is life.

But we need to understand that we have a choice in how we navigate adversity or the unknown.

We can get lost in the wilderness of our fixed and scarcity mindsets around the situation, curl up in a ball, and think, *I can't do this anymore.* Or we can upgrade our inner navigational GPS by thinking, *That didn't go as planned, but I learned a lot from it. Now I can continue my journey toward progress.*

Apply What You've Learned

☐ **Workbook**: Go through this chapter's section in the Leadership on the Rocks workbook.

- ☐ **Mindset**: Reflect on your typical thoughts and reactions to challenging situations. Identify what mindset you usually operate within.
- ☐ **Capture your thoughts**: Create a mantra to say or think that will help you capture your thoughts.
- ☐ **Use EI to reframe your perspective**: Develop a list of questions to ask yourself to reframe your perspective and see the person or situation through another lens.
- ☐ **Wash off the workday**: Establish a routine of actions to help you officially end your workday and clear your mind before you go home to engage with your family and friends.

CHAPTER 4

Identity

The Compass

MY FIRST YEAR in a leadership role was a doozy. Not only was I new to having authority behind my name and decisions, but I was also helping to start an organization from scratch. Forging a path for your leadership sounds exciting. But forging that path while also hiring hundreds of people, building a culture, creating systems and processes, and adding value as a new community establishment? Sheesh!

Like many other professionals, educators have to wear a lot of different hats: teacher, counselor, mediator, entertainer, disciplinarian, data clerk, receptionist, community cheerleader, and even supervisor of "the public" at school events. The workload was so full of competing demands, that I lost myself in the frenzy of it all.

The compass within my internal GPS system had lost its true north, and I felt as though I was spinning in all directions. In trying to be so many things at once, I felt like I didn't know who I was anymore. Without a working internal compass, I couldn't chart a course to forge a clear and confident path in my spinning world.

As we journey through our life and leadership, it is imperative that we protect the head of leadership by ensuring that we always have the working compass of identity in our survival kit. Identity acts as our internal compass that always shows us where our truth north (values, beliefs, and purpose) lies no matter the wilderness situation we are in.

Why Identity Matters

Knowing your identity establishes the cardinal directions for your GPS compass, allowing it to provide a clear direction for where you want to go in life. It also enables you to lead from a place of authentic strength and assurance because you know which way you're headed.

Not knowing who you are, what you believe, or what you're made of keeps the GPS compass spinning and you walking in circles to nowhere.

That's why identity is the first essential resource you must pack and use from your leadership survival kit. It keeps your true north visible and aligns your actions with who you are.

The Leadership on the Rocks Framework defines identity as a set of values, characteristics, traits, and beliefs that are the essence of who the individual (or organization) is.

Without gaining clear direction from a strong and well-defined identity, leaders are susceptible to losing their way in the jungle of competing morals. When you don't put in the work to anchor your sense of identity, you leave yourself vulnerable to spinning out of control and showcasing the worst parts of yourself in difficult situations—precisely when you need to model the best parts of yourself.

The Identity Crisis in Leadership

As people grow through adolescence, it is common for their identity compass to spin in different directions as they work through insecurities to discover who they are. However, identity insecurities don't magically go away as we move out of adolescence and into adulthood. A spinning compass can stay with us for a lifetime if we never work to anchor our identity.

The unfortunate reality is that many people—leaders included—still struggle with an identity crisis. We may be adults, but on the inside, we can still feel like that junior high kid, unsure of who we are as we try to project a polished image to the world (hello, social media filters and the curation of our lives).

As people step into leadership roles, they still carry their internal struggles with them. They can try to hide those identity insecurities by wearing a figurative mask in front of others, but that is never sustainable.

We can't fake our identity by pretending to be something we're not. The stress

Key Takeaway:

Unless you come to terms with your insecurities within your identity, the worst characteristics spawned from those insecurities will manifest and showcase themselves in times of crises, chaos, and conflict.

of maintaining a false front and the anxiety of trying to "not get caught" will eventually break us. It takes an enormous amount of energy to sustain a fake identity, and in the end, the façade always crumbles under pressure.

Guess what leaders deal with on a regular basis? Crises, chaos, and conflict.

Even if you feel confident in your identity, it's crucial to remain vigilant against pride. Digging deep to cultivate humility ensures your confidence doesn't come across as arrogance. The goal is *humble confidence*—being secure in who you are while maintaining genuine humility.

Four Questions for Course Correction

Just like the beloved characters in our favorite books and movies, we all have to work through internal struggles during our leadership journeys. But there's hope!

Your identity is bigger than your feelings in any given moment because who you are is greater than any label, title, mistake, or circumstance you face.

While identity struggles will eventually manifest themselves in times of crises, you can resolve and course correct yourself.

To work through or redefine your identity struggles and thus anchor your leadership compass on your true north, reflect on these four questions. Then respond with the corresponding actions to define or reconcile your values, traits, characteristics, and beliefs.

Question 1: Who do I believe I am?
Action 1: Overcome the past.

Just like you've adopted a mindset (or way of thinking), you also operate out of an identity you've embraced (whether intentionally or unintentionally). You aren't always aware of the labels you've allowed to be placed on your identity and the associations that come with those labels. For example, have you had negative encounters that led you to believe you aren't good enough or that you are unworthy of positive things like love or success?

The goal is to become self-aware and to intentionally identify who you believe you are by naming all the underlying labels and beliefs driving your thoughts and actions. Therefore, you must reflect on, work through, and overcome those lies, stories, pressures, traumas, mindsets, and identity labels you've experienced up to this point in your life.

To do this hard work, consider seeking therapy or diving into your faith. It's not a sign of weakness; it's a path to healing. You'll be able to replace labels and lies with truth and grace.

Question 2: Who do I want to become?
Action 2: Define your aspirational identity.

Once the labels from past beliefs have been revealed, ask yourself who you want to become. This isn't about what kind of leader you want to be or what tasks that person does. Rather, you're defining *who* that aspirational person is at their core and anchoring your internal compass needle on that identity as its north magnetic pole.

You can't jump to *what* or *how* without knowing *who* and *why* first. In his book *The Power to Change*, pastor Craig Groeschel has a powerful mantra for this work: "Who before Do."[8] Identity becomes strongest when we find confidence in *who* we are, not *what* we do. Begin by defining who you want to be as a person and consider the following questions:

Who is someone I admire that I would like to emulate or imitate?
Why do I want to be like this person?
What values, traits, and characteristics does this person embody?
How can I take steps to transform into this person?

Reflect on the kind of heart this person has because from that heart flow thoughts, feelings, and actions. Your heart's condition will be magnified in your behaviors.

Question 3: Do I have what it takes to become who I've longed to be?
Action 3: Focus on progress over perfection.

As you take steps toward becoming who you want to be, you'll inevitably experience moments of doubt and ask yourself, "Do I have what it takes?" Once you start to envision the person you want to become, you'll also notice the gaps between where you are now and where you want to be. This can lead to comparing yourself to others or becoming frustrated at your lack of immediate results.

Personal transformation takes time and consistency, just like a diet plan. There's no quick fix. So when you see the gaps, don't let doubt or fear take over. Instead, focus on progress over perfection. Perfection is not attainable, so let's stop idolizing it and instead celebrate the confidence that comes with steady progress.

Question 4: What roles do I play in helping others discover and build confidence in their identities?
Action 4: Focus on altruism.

The final step is applying your identity work to your leadership. Once you start living in humble confidence of your identity, you'll recognize how many people around you are struggling with their own spinning compasses (identity crises). Noticing and having compassion for others is the heart of a leader.

This compassion will guide you to ask, "What role do I play in helping others discover and build confidence in their identities?"

Here you move to action by focusing on altruism—unselfish concern and care for others. You realize that life isn't about you but about how you can serve others.

As you find your own identity, become a support and encouragement to those who are still searching. Help them see their worth and potential. As you serve others in this way, you'll see your own growth and transformation deepen.

By embracing these four questions and actions, you can begin the journey to not only define your identity to anchor your compass needle but also to become a confident, impactful leader who helps others do the same.

Fixing My Spinning Compass

When it comes to the personal healing of identity, it can seem too hard and abstract. So let me share how I fixed my spinning compass after my first year as an administrator. (Don't worry; I'll hit the highlights!)

Evidence of My Broken Compass

In my late twenties, as I began building my career and raising kids, I felt immense pressure to be perfect—the ideal wife, mom, and professional. Constantly comparing myself to others, I never felt comfortable in my own skin. To hide my insecurities, I focused on image management, and I put on a mask of confidence to avoid judgment. All that internal doubt, shame, guilt, and fear led me into an identity crisis that I tried to cope with by eating and drinking away my emotions.

Seeking Help

The pressure to conform to societal expectations caused great angst and stole my joy. So I made the personal choice to ask God who I truly was and who he meant for me to be. I joined several groups to help me become more self-aware in various aspects of my life, including marriage, parenting, finances, and leadership. The most impactful group I participated in was a Bible study called *Freedom*[9] that focused on finding freedom from the lies I believed about my identity so I could live more truthfully through Christ.

Through daily Bible study and prayer, the GPS through which I viewed the landscape of my life became clearer. During this time, I found the answer to question 1: *Who am I?* I realized that no matter what roles I played, the underlying label driving me was that of a high achiever and people-pleaser who believed I was only loved when achieving or pleasing others.

This mindset led to stress and anxiety as I constantly sought validation. But I overcame these beliefs by understanding that I had trapped myself in a state of pressure and fear.

Anchoring the Compass Needle

My answer to question 2—*Who do I want to be?*—emerged as I leaned more on my faith. I decided I wanted to believe everything God said I was made to be—loved, saved, and a work in progress. I was made to be strong and courageous and to live an abundant life.

Progress over Perfection

Knowing who I wanted to be eventually led to a crisis of belief and question 3: *Do I have what it takes to become who I've longed to be?* As an administrator, I opened a brand-new high school, hired staff, and established a school culture only to face a global pandemic that flipped education on its head within a week. During this chaotic time, I realized that all my self-help books and efforts to implement programs or best practices to "be all I can be" and to "live my best life" didn't give me peace.

Though I don't like hardships, that's where my faith and skills grew. Without challenges and a crisis of belief, I never would have truly found out what I was made of and who I was meant to serve.

Now, on the other side of that crisis, I feel a sweet peace in not being ashamed of where I am on my life journey because I know I'm constantly progressing, and I'll never reach perfection. I learned that while my salvation in Jesus was an instant moment in time, the process of becoming more like him was a lifelong journey. This truth filled me with grace and peace, reminding me it's okay to be a work in progress.

Using My Compass to Help Others

After fixing my compass needle, I have become more humble yet confident in who I am and the leadership abilities God has given me. I'm now focused on answering question 4: *What roles do I play in helping others discover and have confidence in their identities?* That's why I'm writing this book—to help others recognize their potential and make progress on their own transformational journey to become the person (and leader) God is calling them to be.

Today my compass correctly points to my true north (my identity); this allows me to navigate all that life brings my way without losing who I am. And since I no longer feel lost, I experience peace like never before, take risks with confidence, and serve others in ways I never thought possible.

I want this transformation for you too.

Your identity is the compass needle that allows your GPS to correctly guide your every step in the future. Let's make sure your identity is clearly defined and anchored to your north so you can navigate confidently through all the terrain you encounter in your life and leadership.

Values

Now that you have a working compass in your survival kit to always give you the correct cardinal direction for your life and leadership, let's talk about defending it in the presence of threats. The biggest threat to a compass is a differing magnet that can pull the needle away from its established north.

In your life and leadership, all kinds of people will be coming at you like magnets hoping to stick their values and problems to your compass and influence your cardinal directions. To protect your compass from their magnetic draw, you need to know what areas you value most so that as competing values near your compass, you can repel them.

This means you must be intentional in defining not only your identity to establish your true north but the values that you'll live out to protect and defend that identity.

Values are not just a list of words that you like; they govern what you believe and how you behave. Values help define and defend the identity direction you are plotting.

Clear values within your life set the priority for what parts of your life are to be protected and nourished for growth. Without clear values, you are more likely to succumb to the overwhelming magnetic forces besieging you, such as other people's priorities, expectations, and values, as well as societal pressure in general.

Defining Core Values

Unfortunately, many people don't have defined core values for their identity or for their family. Our organizations usually have core values, but two of the most important aspects of one's life (identity and family) are left undefined and exposed to attacks from the outside world. That's not okay. Define what you and your family stand for and then be prepared to live it out and defend it when things of lesser value vie for your time and attention.

Core Values

Core values are the *beliefs, actions, and outcomes* that are most important to you. They are your beliefs that influence your actions. They establish who you are, what you believe, and how you will act and therefore produce the outcomes that are most important to you. They help define your identity so it will be unwavering in a world full of magnets trying to pull you to its ever-changing values.

Decide what your top three or four core values are. Define your belief of what each of those core values means to you and decide the actions you'll take to live them out. Then name what outcomes you should have as a result of those actions.

Below are examples of a core value for my business, family, and self.

An Organization Core Value Example

At BR Essential Services (my leadership coaching business) our core values are written like this: *At BR Essential Services, we RISE to meet the needs of those we serve.*

The acronym RISE stands for the core values of relationships, integrity, service, and essentialism.

Here is an example of our organizational core value of being service focused.

Core Value: Service	
Definition	Service is taking action to help or work for the benefit of others.
Belief	We are to serve others as we would want to be served. "And as you wish that others would do to you, do so to them" (Luke 6:31).

Core Value: Service	
Action	We focus on others' needs by being fully present, listening, observing, understanding, and being quick to respond to their needs.
Outcome	We are people-centered in how we interact and conduct business with others.

A Rees Family Core Value Example

Core Value: Intentional	
Definition	Being intentional means creating thoughts, beliefs, desires, hopes, and actions towards specific goals.
Belief	In all circumstances, we can be deliberate in focusing on and embracing only the things that will add to the mission of significance. "… choose this day whom you will serve… But as for me and my house, we will serve the Lord" (Joshua 24:15).
Action	We will live simply, slowly, and connected by embracing only the things that will add to the mission of significance.
Outcome	We will not be victims of circumstance but will prepare for and have a growth mindset to learn from all situations we encounter.

Bethany's Personal Core Value Example

	Core Value: Essentialism
Definition	Essentialism is focusing on essential rocks that are the basic yet most important building blocks of a fulfilled life.
Belief	When I focus on my highest priorities (essential rocks), it will provide a solid and enriched experience within myself, my relationships, my home, my workplace, and my community. "Finally, brothers, whatever is true, whatever is honorable, whatever is just, whatever is pure, whatever is lovely, whatever is commendable, if there is any excellence, if there is anything worthy of praise, think about these things" (Philippians 4:8).
Action	I am intentional in focusing on what matters most to me (my essential rocks) and will say no to things of lesser value.
Outcome	I will experience harmony between the competing demands of my current responsibilities (self-care, relationships, family, finances, social life, and professional life) without having internal guilt towards the things I said no to.

Now it's your turn to define your values. Without defining them, you will be unprepared to defend them when competing priorities come your way.

So go download the free workbook and get to work defining what you, your family, or your organization values. Don't forget to define it, identify the belief behind it, list what actions you'll take to live it out, and name what outcomes you'll have as a result.

Mantras

As you use your compass of identity to establish direction for your journey in life and leadership, march forward with a cadence to keep you focused.

One of the many lessons I have learned over the years is that while I can't seem to remember the details of my calendar or even what I came into my office for, I can still sing the jingles of commercials from my childhood.

Why?

Our brains love simplicity.

There's a reason that most advertisements have a tagline or jingle—it's easy to remember and it reminds us of the bigger concept.

Even though you have learned a lot about using the rock of identity as a compass to anchor your direction and core values to protect it from competing forces, chances are that you can forget about how to use your compass tomorrow. We don't want that to happen. Thus, one very important strategy to help you stay focused on using your compass is to take your leader mindset and values or tenets (beliefs or principles) that define your identity and develop mantras that you can remember.

Mantras are simply statements or slogans repeated frequently, and when marching towards your desired destination, you will need them!

There is so much power in developing mantras for your life and leadership. It helps you with

- mental health and self-talk (capturing those thoughts),
- relationships and communication (finding new perspectives), and

IDENTITY

- goals that you want to reach (providing clarity).

By creating easy-to-repeat mantras, you are creating reminders for yourself, your family, or your team at work. These short sayings are not only easy to remember and repeat, but the beauty is that they represent a larger, more complex concept without having to use a lot of words.

These mantras also become marching cadences and battle cries to protect your head of leadership by focusing on what matters most (your essential rocks) when chaos surrounds you. You will come to depend heavily on your mantras as reminders for using your compass to anchor your thoughts and guide your decisions instead of being attracted to the dangerous pull of the world around you.

Here are some of my favorites to help me remember *who* I am (identity), *how* I choose to think (mindset), and other tenets (principles) that I value.

Mantras

- "I am worthy." (Identity)
- "I am a work in progress." (Identity)
- "I do the right thing until I feel the right thing." (Identity and Mindset)
- "Don't tell myself a story." (Mindset)
- "What can I learn from this?" (Mindset)
- "Be quick to listen and slow to speak." (Principle: Focus on others before self.)
- "Rocks over sand." (Principle: Don't sweat the small stuff.)
- "Culture over strategy." (Principle: People over product.)

Now I want to challenge you. Do you have mantras that you live and work by?

If not, create them to anchor your thoughts, guide your actions, and rally your energy when you start to feel bombarded with pressures to wander off course.

If you do already have mantras, then assess whether or not you need to update them based on the current pressures around you. Life and work tend to have various seasons that we live through; you need to make sure you have mantras to match the season you're in.

By establishing your identity as your "true north" and protecting it with clearly defined values and mantras, you'll develop a strong compass for your internal GPS that will always guide you in the right direction. In your leadership survival kit, always carry the compass of identity.

Apply What You've Learned

- ☐ **Workbook**: Go through this chapter's section in the Leadership on the Rocks workbook.
- ☐ **Identity**: Work through the 4 questions and actions to help you define your identity.
  - ☐ Question 1: Who do I believe I am?
  - ☐ Action 1: Overcome the past.
  - ☐ Question 2: Who do I want to become?
  - ☐ Action 2: Define your aspirational identity.
  - ☐ Question 3: Do I have what it takes to become who I've longed to be?

- ☐ Action 3: Focus on progress over perfection.
- ☐ Question 4: What roles do I play in helping others discover and build confidence in their identities?
- ☐ Action 4: Focus on altruism.
- ☐ **Core values:** Decide what your top three or four core values are and clarify them.
  - ☐ Define your belief of what that core value means to you.
  - ☐ Decide the actions you'll take to live them out.
  - ☐ Name what outcome you should have as a result of those actions.
- ☐ **Mantras**: Create mantras as reminders and battle cries to stay focused on your identity, purpose, core values, principles, projects, or strategies.

CHAPTER 5

Purpose

The Map

HAVING INSOMNIA-FILLED NIGHTS was not a bonus experience I expected to come with a promotion. As I would lay wide awake, there were two questions I kept asking myself: *Why? How?* I had unpacked my own compass of identity and knew the kind of person I wanted to be, but I didn't know why I still felt so lost in my life and leadership role. It finally came to me: I knew who I was but didn't know where I wanted to go, why I was going, or how I was going to get there.

My head of leadership had clear thinking (mindset) and humble confidence (identity), but it still didn't have clear direction. And that's when I realized that I needed a map to define the what, why, and how of my journey.

Purpose is that map. Here's what that means and how to pull it from your survival kit.

What Is Purpose?

We love using the GPS maps on our smartphones to help us navigate the roads. To use this beloved tool, we have to enter the specific destination so we can access an accurate map to follow. But more than that, we have to know why we are going to that destination in the first place. Doing the *what* (traveling) by following the *how* (directions) without knowing the *why* (reason) lacks a big piece of the puzzle.

It's natural to desire meaning in our lives and work. This is why we need clear purpose. Having purpose gives you a path to follow and helps you anticipate what lies ahead.

The Leadership on the Rocks Framework defines purpose as the reason you exist, your mission to carry out.

Purpose is tied to your beliefs and is shared through your calling (how you engage with the world). Discovering and becoming confident in your purpose will give you an accurate map to follow throughout your life and leadership, ensuring you never get lost while carrying out your mission. It keeps you from getting distracted by the day-to-day minutiae—those side trips that steal away productivity.

You have unique gifts and passions that, when aligned with a strong purpose, will change your world and the world around you. Yes, you, my friend, have a God-given purpose and are destined to positively impact many lives!

People are born with an innate desire to be on a mission and fulfill a purpose bigger than themselves. Organizations are created to solve problems, champion causes, and serve stakeholders. But when people and organizations forget their reason for existence, they lose the drive to face each day, becoming passive participants in their own lives.

Living Intentionally

There's a quote I love from Michael Gerber in his book *The E Myth Revisited*.

> I believe it's true that the difference between great people and everyone else is that great people create their lives actively, while everyone else is created by their lives, passively waiting to see where life takes them next. The difference between the two is the difference between living fully and just existing. The difference between the two is living intentionally and living by accident.[10]

We are meant to live and work intentionally, but many people merely exist, letting life happen to them. Instead of leading, planning, and living into their purpose, they're waiting for others' expectations to create their lives.

This is backwards! We should want to be active participants in our lives, intentionally living into our purpose on purpose. A lack of mission not only affects our careers, but it also impacts our physical and mental health.

In Japan, the concept of purpose is called *ikigai* (pronounced ick-ee-guy) or "reason for being." It isn't tied to grand achievements but is found in the humble actions of everyday life. This focus on purpose has led regions like Okinawa, Japan, to produce numerous centenarians (people living over 100 years).[11]

Isn't that beautiful?

Chasing

There is so much pressure in this world to veer off course by chasing every rabbit trail you see on your journey through life. However, rabbit trails—busyness, striving, or running after the newest shiny widget and trend in hopes of increasing your status—are not the paths you are called to take. In fact, they are what cause you to ask, "How did I get here?" when you finally realize how off course you are.

Your journey to fulfilling your purpose will be peppered with many distractions. One of the biggest distractions is the comparison game.

We often compare ourselves to others for validation—to see if we "matter" or are "winning" in life. We also compare the reality we're actually living to our own concept of the ideal life.

Comparison is the thief of joy!

Key Takeaway:

Your purpose is bigger than your job, title, or paycheck.

Another rabbit trail that is taken often is constantly seeking the "right job." How did we start confusing our job titles with the fulfillment of our life's purpose? That's bad thinking!

A custodian's job doesn't carry less purpose or meaning than that of a doctor. Without either of these important positions, we would have to live uncomfortably among all the self-imposed trash we create in our spaces and put in our bodies.

You can fulfill your purpose no matter your job, title, or circumstance. So check your heart's motivation: Are you chasing titles, paychecks, or status because you think they will fill your need for purpose and worth?

Chasing after these things won't bring you peace and fulfillment in your life; it will keep you running from one achievement to the next, always seeking validation.

It's crucial to identify your personal purpose so that before job titles and paychecks come—or when they change—you can stand firm knowing that your existence is about more than your job title or paycheck.

To stop the chasing of rabbit trails of meaning, you have to let go of the expectations you have about the title or paycheck you're "supposed" to have by now. Instead of looking left or right for validation, look up and within to discover your true purpose and identity.

You're not made to be like anyone else, and you're not made to follow anyone else's exact path. You have unique gifts and talents that make you valuable wherever you serve; this, in turn, helps you to know *why* you serve. When you know your *why*, you'll always have a mapped route to get where you want to go.

Let me share how I discovered my personal purpose—a purpose that goes beyond any job title I could ever have.

Finding My Purpose

I thought I was born to teach high school history—until everything changed. After six years in education, I moved to Texas and took the only teaching-related job still available in July: an instructional technologist role. Instead of engaging with students, I found myself fixing teachers' computers and managing software. It felt far removed from what I believed I was meant to do.

Here's how that conversation with God went.

Excuse me God, but apparently you didn't get the script I wrote for my life.

Do you want me to send you another copy via prayer mail?

Why are you laughing, God?

Oh, you have better plans for how you want me to serve you and others?

Ugh. I'd rather not.

Trust you?

Okay fine, let's do it your way.

I found my purpose when I stopped fighting God for the life story I thought I should have and started growing where he planted me.

What I learned during this transition was that my purpose wasn't tied to a specific content, age-group, or even industry. God put me in situations I didn't want to be in to humble me, teach me new skills, and prepare me for the next assignment. When I stopped focusing on myself and started noticing the people and situations in my path, my heart began to break for what was missing and to flutter with excitement about how I could help. It was in this blend of broken-heartedness and excitement that I found my calling.

I've discovered that challenging situations open our eyes and transform our hearts. When we notice something missing or feel stirred by the possibility of making a difference, we usually discover our God-given purpose.

The insights, experiences, and skills we gain in difficult seasons will shape us and clarify our individual calling—our *why* behind our *what*.

Finding Your Purpose

As you land in your own wilderness of life and leadership, it's important to unpack and use this tool. Here are four steps to discover your map of purpose through your calling.

Step 1: Define your identity.

We already talked a lot about identity, so I'll just reinforce the point that having clear values, characteristics, traits, and beliefs makes sure the compass on the map is facing the right direction. When the compass knows where north is, it allows the map to create the accurate routes of action to get where you want to go.

Step 2: Know your strengths and constraints.

It's hard to find your calling when you aren't sure about your gifts, talents, and abilities, so reflect on your strengths and constraints.

Your strengths are the qualities that help you succeed and lead effectively.

Think about talents that come naturally or areas where people frequently compliment you. (And I don't just mean talent as in playing a sport or an instrument or even winning at trivia night in your local bar. Dive deeper than that.)

For example, I am good at brainstorming and creative problem-solving. This serves me well when encouraging and coaching individuals or teams as they work through problems. Where they tend to see no solution, I usually see a lot of them.

Look at the example chart below. Do any of these come naturally to you?

ARE YOU ABLE TO:

- rally a team
- connect with emotions
- teach others
- comfort the hurting
- creatively solve problems
- organize chaos
- host events
- be a listening ear
- make people feel welcomed
- create beautiful designs
- coach and encourage others
- cook meals
- provide analytical analysis
- fight for justice
- connect the dots (bring ideas/people together)

Write down your strengths.

Now that you have a list of how awesome you are, I hate to pop your bubble, but your awesomeness can be taken too far. If taken too far, our strengths can sometimes hurt our team. This is where the eye rolls start with "oh, here she/he goes again with…"

It's important to not only identify our strengths but to also go deeper with two more substeps:

- Identify how our strengths could be taken too far.
- Define actions we can take to keep them in check.

For example, my strength in brainstorming sometimes overwhelms my team if I don't preface ideas with, "We're not implementing everything—this is just to spark creativity." This one little disclaimer eases the stress of others and also reminds me to chill out with the brainstorming.

Learning not to go overboard with your strengths prevents unintended negative impacts on others. How can you safeguard your strengths to keep them in check?

On the flip side, your constraints are qualities that act as limitations. While you can improve in these areas, it's essential to recognize that they don't disqualify you from leadership. They keep you humble as you recognize you always have something to learn and work on.

Now think about some constraints you have. Do you have limitations that frustrate you? Do you have blind spots in the way you do, see, or think about things?

As we did with our strengths, we need to define actions we can take to keep our constraints in check.

For instance, my tendency to people-please means I often agree to too many things, leading me to be overwhelmed. By acknowledging this, I can create strategies, like pausing before responding, to help grow in this area.

Know your constraints because if you stay blind to them or ignore them, they can cause absolute havoc with you and your team.

Identifying both strengths and constraints provides valuable self-awareness. By knowing what you tend to bring to the table, you can better discover what you were meant to do and, even better, what you weren't meant to do. This will help you later on in hiring as you look to build a team of people with diverse skills.

Step 3: Dream again.
Develop a vision for a better future!

Vision inspires hope and motivates you through tough times. Take a moment to dream again about a better future for your life, home, and work. Consider what problems you've noticed and what breaks your heart or fires you up.

For example, as I worked with students and teachers, I noticed a lack of encouragement and leadership that broke my heart. I started to dream about what it would look like if people were equipped to lead and empowered to serve, no matter their circumstances. These dreams shaped my vision of cultivating strong, compassionate leaders in families, organizations, and communities.

Ask yourself: What problems do I notice? What would the world be like if they were solved? Your answers will provide insight into your unique calling and how you can serve.

Step 4: Project and protect your purpose.
The final step is to project (display) and protect (defend) your purpose. You have unique gifts to share, but too often we disqualify ourselves by never exhibiting them for others to see. Time and time again, I have seen people who notice something and yet say nothing. Don't disqualify the importance of your insight and gifts, no matter the room you are sitting in. Extend your influence by sharing your observations, knowledge, and skills with others.

Whether it's your time, attention, heart, or wallet, something or someone is always out to rob you of it. Don't let comparison rob you of worth. Don't let fear rob you of courage. Don't let doubt rob you of action.

Protect your gifts by living them out, not hiding them. You were made for this moment. Embrace your purpose and go serve others with confidence!

By following these four steps—defining your identity, knowing your strengths and constraints, dreaming again, and projecting and protecting your purpose—you can discover and live out your calling with clarity and intention.

Organizational Purpose

As a leader, you have a personal purpose, but if you represent an organization, it's crucial to be a great steward of its purpose as well. Employees need to know why their job matters, why the company matters, and how it makes the world a better place by serving its stakeholders the way it does. Without a clear purpose, people, teams, and organizations wander and work aimlessly, leading to decreased results.

Leadership expert Simon Sinek explains in *Start with Why*. "Knowing your WHY is not the only way to be successful, but it is the only way to maintain a lasting success and have a greater blend of innovation and flexibility."[12]

When organizations and their employees are deeply connected to their *why*, they are protected from burnout while becoming more innovative and adaptable.

Purpose becomes the mission and vision that guide our work. It is our map, ensuring each group understands why they exist and where they are headed. They need to know the mission to guide their actions and the vision for what they are working towards.

People often confuse mission and vision. Mission is the purpose and why you exist, while vision is your hope for the future—the destination you are heading toward. Together, they provide clarity for the desired routes on your map.

Mission: The Why Behind the What

Mission is the "why" behind your "what"—the purpose behind daily actions. To understand mission and purpose, let's talk about work. Most organizations have a mission statement, but it is rarely discussed or tied to a higher purpose that motivates people. Without a clear mission, employees don't know the "why behind the what" of their work.

As Blanchard, Hodges, and Hendry emphasize in their book *Lead Like Jesus*, "an effective mission statement should express a higher purpose for the greater good and give meaning to the efforts of each individual in the organization."[13]

How many of us know and see the higher purpose within our career? How many of us even know our organization's mission statement? My guess is very few.

When asked what business they're in, most people respond with a generic career category: "I'm in marketing. I'm in retail. I'm in education." These answers lack passion and purpose. We need to go beyond these categories and dive deeper into the true purpose behind what we do.

Take Chick-fil-A, for example. While they're technically in the chicken and fast-food business, their mission is clear: "To glorify God by being a faithful steward of all that is entrusted to us. To have a positive influence on all who come in contact with Chick-fil-A."[14]

From the moment you step into one of their restaurants, you feel the difference in how you are served as a guest. They've tied their mission to a higher purpose that guides everything they do.

My company, BR Essential Services, might be classified in the self-improvement industry. However, our purpose is about building strong leadership at every level of interaction. We are truly in the business of developing leaders who make a positive impact at work and at home.

So let me ask you again: What business are you in? Do you have a clear mission and purpose for what you do and what your organization does?

If not, and you're the leader, you need to stop right now and clarify your purpose. Make it tied to that higher purpose that everyone is motivated by. Don't just print it on a poster or slap it on a wall. Your mission is something you talk about, teach to your team, and live out constantly. It is showcased the most by how people engage with one another. Every action your organization takes should be directly tied to achieving the mission.

If you're an employee and your organization lacks a clear mission, start the conversation by advocating for clarity. It is imperative that you know your purpose within the organization so you know what you are working for beyond the paycheck. Be intentional in clarifying and referring to your purpose because it's the map that directs everything you do.

Vision: Where You're Going

When it comes to purpose, you may know why you exist, but if you don't know where you're headed, you can still end up feeling lost. Everyone needs to know where they're going.

Vision is the destination—the future you're striving to create. Vision is what the future will look like if you fully live out your mission. Even organizations need to dream again. Once the organization knows its purpose and commits to its mission, it needs to visualize what the future would look like if the mission were fulfilled.

The Alzheimer's Association's vision is "a world without Alzheimer's disease."[15]

My company's dream is that every family, team, department, and organization will have quality leaders who steward those they serve.

At the high school I helped open, our vision was about growing future citizens. We dreamed that by the time students left our campus, they would be equipped with skills and empowered with purpose to impact the community. Such a vision is not just about today but about the hope of who our students could become.

Visualization is a powerful tool when it comes to connecting with your vision. It helps you see where you're going and keeps hope alive for a better future, even during tough times. The vision provides a bright light through the darkest of challenges. If the organization stops dreaming of a better future, it stops growing. And when something stops growing, it starts dying.

Tying Purpose, Mission, and Vision Together

Leaders must ensure that mission and vision are not just words on paper but a clear map that directs every step of the organization. They should inspire people to see the bigger picture and align their work with the organization's goals. Employees who connect with the mission and see the vision are more engaged, motivated, and committed to making a meaningful impact.

Your organization's mission and vision can create that sense of purpose that people crave by giving them a clear direction to a desired destination. Purpose is the difference between employees who just show up at a j-o-b for a paycheck and those who show up with passion, ready to make a difference.

With a clear mission and vision map in your leadership survival kit, you and your organization can achieve more than you ever imagined.

In writing this chapter on purpose, I am reminded of this truth: Our world landscape is changing rapidly.

While the trends and technologies of the world evolve, our purpose holds firm. Our map of purpose doesn't ever get thrown away; it gets upgraded to provide even more clarity about why we exist and what we wish to accomplish.

The leaders and organizations who understand this will continue to thrive. The others will not. Pack your map of purpose, and you'll always know which way to go.

Apply What You've Learned

- ☐ **Workbook**: Go through this chapter's section in the Leadership on the Rocks workbook.
- ☐ **Define your Identity**: If you haven't already, go back and do the work in chapter 4 by answering the four questions of identity.
- ☐ **Strengths:** List your strengths. Identify how they could be taken too far. Then define actions you can take to keep them in check.
- ☐ **Constraints**: List your constraints. Identify how they could be taken too far. Then define actions you can take to free (or grow) your constraints; this includes hiring people that have strengths where you have constraints.
- ☐ **Dream again**: Brainstorm and list what you notice at work (or in the world) that breaks your heart. Write what the future would look like if those problems were solved. Brainstorm and list what gets you excited to work or serve.
- ☐ **Mission**: Write your personal mission statement (why you exist and what you bring to the world).

PURPOSE

- ☐ **Vision**: Describe your personal vision for what you want your life, your career, etc. to look like in the future because you have lived out your personal mission.
- ☐ **Organizational mission/vision:** Seek clarity on what your organization's mission and vision are and how your work is tied to them.

PART 3

The Heart of Leadership

The Lifeblood of Connection

CHAPTER 6
Relationships

Vital Nutrients

A SAD TRUTH THAT I hate to admit is that as a former educator, I have had to de-escalate a lot of altercations—student to student, teacher to teacher, and even parents to teachers or coaches. Most of the time, de-escalation techniques worked to end the feud.

However, in one instance, as I was providing supervision during the lunch period, I noticed the body language of two students in line, and I could tell things were getting heated. I stepped in between them to ask if each student was okay or needed assistance. As I turned my body to listen to one of them, the other launched over my shoulder to deliver what could only be described as a Superman punch to the face of the student talking to me. In the chaos, I fell down, and the fight ensued on top of me until I managed to crawl out and get back on my feet.

Of course, other administrators swooped in to assist me in pulling the students apart. We removed both students from the public location and into separate offices, and I chose to stay with the would-be mixed martial arts fighter.

As I sat with him, I introduced myself and asked him to share what was going on. He had only been a student on our campus for a week and felt like he needed to establish dominance to avoid being disrespected. In that moment, I realized the heart of the problem wasn't just his actions—it was the absence of a positive connection. He didn't yet have a relationship with an adult or peer, and he wasn't familiar with the culture of respect we had worked hard to build in our school.

While we still followed proper protocols and consequences, I made it my mission to engage with him differently. I greeted him by name, asked about his interests, and consistently checked in with him. Over time, those intentional efforts built trust and respect, and I saw a profound change in the way he interacted with others.

This experience reinforced an important lesson: relationships are the life-giving nutrients of any thriving culture, whether it's in a school, workplace, or leadership setting.

The Survival Connection

Just like nutrients sustain life in the wilderness, relationships sustain the heart of leadership. Without healthy connections, teams feel like they don't have the energy to move forward. A strong leader understands that they are in the people business—connecting with and rallying individuals into a cohesive, high-performing team united by a common goal.

Whether we find ourselves wandering aimlessly or intentionally forging a path in the rocky terrain of leadership, one thing is certain—the quickest way to end your journey is for you and your team to feel like you have to "go it alone." Like nutrients, relationships are essential to survival; without them, leaders and teams alike will wither under the strain of the journey.

The Culture Connection

Relationships are the force shaping your leadership culture. Just as the nourishment you provide your body determines its health, the quality of the relationships you build determines the health of your organization's culture. A thriving culture cannot exist without the steady nutrients of connection and trust. While tasks, systems, and processes are vital, they are not the most important aspect of leadership—the people are.

Every interaction you have with your team either energizes or depletes the trust and connection you've built. John Maxwell said it best in *The 21 Irrefutable Laws of Leadership*: "Everything rises and falls on leadership."[16] The quality of a leader determines the success of the people they lead. Managers who only focus on tasks risk running their team dry, while leaders who prioritize people—listening to their ideas, supporting their goals, and fostering their growth—create thriving ecosystems where everyone flourishes.

If you want to be a leader who makes a positive impact, start with building better relationships. The flow of connection doesn't just sustain you; it keeps your team alive, vibrant, and ready to tackle the challenges ahead.

Why Relationships Matter

The quality of our relationships directly affects our overall performance. While individuals are responsible for their behavior regardless of the situation, the relationship they have with "the boss" significantly impacts their attitude and motivation.

In leadership, people are both your greatest asset and your greatest responsibility. Understanding how we connect with one another is imperative because, like nutrients in the wilderness, relationships are the resource that sustains our quality of life and work. Without them, leaders and their teams dry up, losing the motivation required to move forward.

Leadership is not merely a title or level of authority; it is about influence. The most positive influence comes from building strong relationships with others. People are most inspired by leaders they trust, admire, and see as worthy of following. Just as nutrients revive the weary, relationships invigorate the heart of your leadership and the strength of your team.

This means that at work, a person can be in charge but not be considered a leader at all. These people are managers. The concept of managing, or being a manager, is all about controlling the inputs to accomplish an output. While managing as a skill is important for maintaining order, it shouldn't be a desired leadership style because it often overlooks the people involved in the processes.

Managers are task focused, and leaders are people focused.

In leadership, prioritizing people over tasks is crucial. Relationships are what provide the foundation and sustenance needed in the often challenging terrain of leadership. Unfortunately, we sometimes view people as obstacles hindering our ability to complete tasks. When we prioritize tasks over relationships, it's akin to neglecting the very nutrients that keep everyone united and thriving.

As leaders, we must recognize that we are in the people business and must therefore nourish the heart of our leadership body. The interactions between people—the relationships—are at the heart of effective leadership, serving as the essential nutrients of organizational health and success.

Just as the right nutrients are essential for survival, relationships demand intentional effort and nurturing. Regardless of the challenges a person may present, they deserve to be nourished with value, respect, and dignity. Valuing others is fundamental to building meaningful connections.

The Thing About Relationships

We need deep, meaningful relationships for mental survival just as much as we need nutrients for physical survival in the wilderness. Strong relationships don't build themselves—they require intentionality, effort, and the right resources. Similarly, relationships grow stronger when we are mindful of what we bring to them. We must tend to our relationships with qualities like selfless love, focus, empathy, listening, and support. These are the elements that help nourish relationships.

But just as relationships can falter when we bring the wrong materials—pride, arrogance, distractedness, apathy, disregard, and opposition—effective leadership depends on tending to our relationships with care and respect. To build a leadership culture that thrives, we must avoid behaviors that diminish connection and instead focus on actions that sustain and strengthen it.

It's also important to acknowledge that not every relationship will flourish. In the wilderness of leadership, some connections may not develop as expected. Not everyone will like you, and that's okay. What matters is that you've done your best to nurture the right relationships and foster positive connections.

Before we delve into specific strategies for cultivating healthy relationships, let's start with an understanding of the basic psychological factors impacting people and their connections. Just as a skilled camper knows what ingredients will nourish or poison them, leaders must grasp the universal principles behind what properly feeds relationship building. While our goal isn't to become psychologists, it is important to understand and act upon these principles to ensure that the relationships continue to provide the strength and support our teams need to thrive.

Why "The Psychology" Matters

As Dave Ramsey famously said, "Leading your business is easy… until people get involved."[17] I would broaden that sentiment: The work is easy until people are involved. While tasks can be complex, they are not as intricate as people. This complexity often leads many in leadership positions to focus on tasks (emails, presentations, reports, etc.) and avoid people and the interpersonal dynamics at play.

Serving and leading a diverse group of people, personalities, and skill sets may seem challenging, but leaders can build positive relationships with all types by understanding the basic psychological needs and motivations of their team members. People are driven by fundamental needs that influence how they work and interact.

To understand human motivation, we can look at the work of psychologist Abraham Maslow who outlined that people's basic needs must be met before they can reach their full potential. At the foundation are physiological needs like food, water, and shelter. Once these are satisfied, people seek safety, followed by belonging—feeling accepted and valued by others.

From there, the need for esteem arises—the desire for recognition and to feel that one adds value. Finally, at the top is self-actualization where individuals strive to become their best selves.[18] While theories like Maslow's have evolved, the underlying principles of human motivation remain constant.

Key Takeaway:

People need to feel safe, valued, and connected to thrive.

At the core, individuals want to feel safe, valued, and connected. This psychological truth should be the foundation of your leadership approach because these needs impact how your team members show up in the workplace and how they perform.

If these emotional needs go unmet, employees may have the potential, but without the support they need, they're unable to perform at their best. It's like high-performance athletes without the proper nourishment—they can't compete effectively without the right fuel to energize their bodies.

However, when a leader focuses on nurturing relationships—acknowledging the importance of emotional safety, belonging, and respect—they foster a culture of trust and collaboration that strengthens athletes and therefore the whole team.

Often, individuals fail to reach their full leadership potential because they neglect or even avoid the psychology of relationship building. Don't be an avoider! Leaders must resist the temptation to rely solely on authority and task management and instead invest in their team's psychological well-being. The best leaders understand that strong relationships are key to motivation and success.

Therefore, as a leader you need to be aware of and invest time in the psychology behind relationship building, or you will always be burned by it. Bad or weak relationships create a workplace culture riddled with mistrust, conflict, drama, and subpar results. This scenario is a recipe for disaster—and a disaster is not your desired outcome.

In essence, leaders who meet their team's needs for belonging and esteem are not just supervising employees; they're creating an environment where individuals can flourish and contribute meaningfully. Focusing on this foundational aspect of leadership leads to a healthy, productive workplace culture.

When we intentionally build positive relationships, our work culture becomes more resilient and better equipped to handle problems, conflicts, or constraints. Above all, focusing on people and nurturing positive relationships is essential because employees are a leader's greatest resource—and also the source of most of your heartburn and heartache.

Make People a Priority

While there are many ways to meet the psychological needs of others, let's just start with the most basic strategy to nourish the relationships within your team: make people a priority.

What you schedule reflects what you prioritize—period. If people need to feel safe, valued, and connected to be motivated, ensure your calendar makes time for them.

Spending time with your employees not only strengthens relationships but also provides valuable insights into how to lead them effectively. Time invested with your team will reveal their work styles and the support they need to excel. To learn more about the people you serve, consider the following approaches:

- Assess personality types as a general gauge of how individuals think and work.
- Spend time getting to know them both professionally and personally.

For this reason, I love scheduling one-on-ones to check in on people. It is honestly one of the highlights of my day. I also love hosting social events to get to know my teams outside of work, and I'm intentional about making some events family friendly. Planning a team-building event where we learn about each other's personalities and how each of us ticks, works, and communicates always enriches our relationships.

Focusing on people and all the complexities that come with the human race matters! Brené Brown says it best in her book *Dare to Lead*.

"Leaders must either *invest* a reasonable amount of time attending to fears and feelings, or *squander* an unreasonable amount of time trying to manage ineffective and unproductive behavior (emphasis added)."[19]

If you don't invest in relationships and leading people, you'll spend all your time managing ineffective and unproductive behavior.

Remember, managers focus on tasks; leaders focus on people. So who or what receives most of your attention—emails or people?

Understand and Anticipate Needs

Now that we've explored the importance of relationships and the psychology behind them, let's dive into how to read the room and truly connect with your team.

Building meaningful relationships doesn't require being a counselor or a genius, but it does take emotional intelligence and the practice of noticing. To connect effectively, you need to be intentional about observing, learning, and asking questions to uncover the needs, thoughts, and emotions of the people around you.

While it's important not to make snap judgments, leaders must actively seek to understand what motivates their team members, what challenges they face, and what they value most. This awareness allows you to move beyond assumptions and engage authentically with others, fostering trust and connection.

Let's illustrate this idea with a common leadership scenario: being hired as the new leader of a team and creating a first impression.

First Impressions

I love the adage "an ounce of prevention is worth a pound of cure" because it's so true. When it comes to building positive relationships, we could tweak it to fit. An ounce of a great first impression is worth a pound of therapy for the conflicts you'll avoid.

When you step into a new leadership role, there's always that first encounter with the team after you've been named "in charge." While you may feel excited and ready to dive in, your team's feelings and expectations are already in motion long before your arrival.

Even before you officially join the team, they've started crafting stories about you. These stories, whether grounded in fact or speculation, influence their expectations of your leadership. When a team learns they're losing their current boss and gaining a new one, it often triggers fear and anxiety. Even if they disliked their previous leader, the saying "better the devil you know than the devil you don't" applies. People fear the unknown and dread change, leading to all manner of thoughts that may be indicative of deeper feelings:

Oh great, now I have to prove myself as a great employee to the new boss. (Desire to be seen and valued for their contributions.)

I'm so tired of change and transitions. Thank God I only have three more years until retirement. (Longing for stability.)

Ugh, I wonder what idea the new leader is going to come up with that's going to create more busywork for me. (Frustration with previous experiences of unnecessary changes.)

Just when I finally felt our team was in a groove, here we go getting a new boss. (Desire for what is familiar and a dislike of change.)

This new manager better fix all these problems we've been dealing with forever, or I'm out of here. (Expectation that the new leader will resolve long-standing issues.)

I heard they hired Bethany as our new manager, and somebody's brother's cousin told me she fired a whole department at her last company. (Anxiety that the negative rumors are true.)

The anxiety surrounding leadership transitions can be so palpable it can feel as if the room is holding its breath, weighed down by unspoken words. This underscores the critical importance of first impressions when stepping into a leadership role.

To help you better understand how learning about and responding to your team's needs can shape first impressions, let me share a tale of two managers.

Manager One's First Impression

Manager one walks into the team meeting with the big boss. He sits beside the big boss at the conference table and has sidebar conversations with him as employees arrive. During the whole introduction meeting, he looks only at the big boss and maintains a serious expression. When introduced, his tone is polished but serious, and he talks about his past successes as though he needs everyone to know his entire resume. He ends his long speech about himself with a statement about being excited to lead the team and produce results.

Manager Two's First Impression

Manager two walks into the room with the big boss but intentionally places his things away from the big boss. He greets each employee at the door with a smile and handshake as they come in. When the meeting starts, he takes his place among the team members. While the big boss speaks, he acknowledges team members' glances with a smile and nod. Upon introduction, he smiles and makes eye contact, speaking in a positive tone. He begins by expressing excitement about joining their team, praises their previous accomplishments, and mentions that he looks forward to one-on-one meetings with each team member. He emphasizes family and work-life harmony and concludes by reminding everyone of their greater purpose.

Which manager gave the better first impression?

Manager two, right? He took time to reflect on and anticipate the team's feelings. Thus, he greeted them warmly and sat amongst them.

His introductory speech focused on praising the team to put their inner feelings and thoughts at ease rather than promoting himself. He also explained his first action as manager: prioritizing getting to know them individually through one-on-ones. This allows him to move from anticipating and assumptions to knowing and understanding.

First impressions set the tone for a relationship, and once opinions are formed, they can be incredibly difficult to change.

By seeking out and empathizing with (or at minimum, proactively anticipating) people's thoughts and feelings, your demeanor, approach, and communication with them will invite more positive connections.

If you are intentional in focusing on the team's questions, thoughts, and feelings during your first impression, you'll be significantly ahead in building positive relationships with your team. Making a great first impression is an investment you can't afford to miss.

Relationships and Culture

When our leadership team opened a new high school from scratch, we had a rare and exciting opportunity to build a culture entirely from the ground up. It was more than just creating a mission statement or vision. We were intentional to go deeper by defining who we were and how we would engage with one another.

We were deliberate about clarifying our core beliefs, the behaviors that would bring those beliefs to life, and the kind of common language we would use to ensure alignment. As a larger educator team, we carefully designed traditions that would unite us and celebrations that would inspire us. By doing this, we didn't just outline what we hoped our culture would be; we built it, brick by brick, through intentional actions.

This approach necessitated more than words on paper. It required us to model, reinforce, and defend the values we claimed to uphold. As we laid this cultural foundation, we discovered the profound truth that relationships are the life-giving nutrients of any thriving culture. They are the source of its strength and the quickest way to poison or heal it.

Without intentionality, relationships can drift into patterns that harm the group rather than nurture it. Management consultant, educator, and author Peter Drucker is often attributed with this famous leadership quote: "Culture eats strategy for breakfast."[20] The intent behind this often-quoted phrase is that you can come up with the best strategy on how to move your team forward, but the culture in which that strategy is embedded decides whether or not that strategy will be successful.

Leaders who take purposeful steps to shape the culture they desire create an environment where teams not only function but flourish no matter the strategy or initiative implemented. This work begins with three critical actions: defining the line, coaching the line, and defending the line.

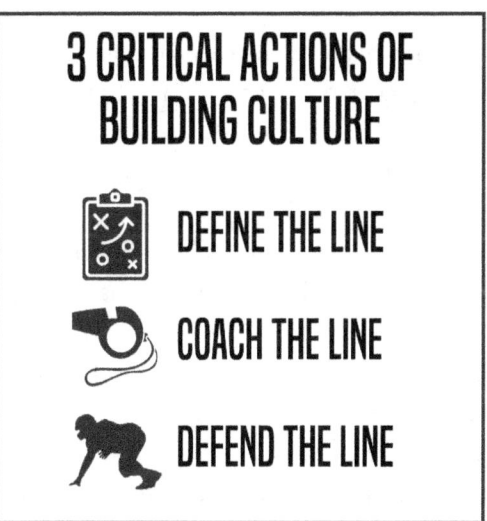

Define the Line

In survival scenarios, understanding your environment is crucial. Whether you're navigating a dense forest, crossing a desert, or scaling a mountain, survival begins with defining the boundaries of where you are and what you need to thrive. This process is much like establishing the cultural "line" for your own team.

The first step is to map the terrain by defining who you are as a group, what you believe, and how you operate. Like marking safe zones or mapping resources in the wild, you must clearly articulate your team's purpose, values, and norms. Symbols, shared language, and rituals act as landmarks, giving your team direction and a sense of identity.

Without this clarity, your team is like a group of hikers wandering without a map or compass. By intentionally defining the cultural line, you provide the structure and sense of purpose that keeps everyone moving toward a common goal.

Coach the Line

Once the boundaries of the terrain become clear, survival depends on teaching the group how to engage within it. In the wild, this means showing others how to use a compass, read the stars, and build a fire. In leadership, it means coaching your team to embody the values and behaviors that sustain a positive culture.

This is the ongoing process of teaching and reinforcing cultural norms. As Seth Godin would say, "People like us do things like this."[21] Modeling expected behaviors, offering feedback, and encouraging reflection are like providing essential survival skills. They ensure that your team can navigate challenges and stay aligned with the established cultural line.

Much like a survival guide showing a group how to set up camp, leaders must offer consistent support and guidance. Without this coaching, even the clearest map will go unused, and the team will falter.

Defend the Line

In survival situations, one of the greatest threats is not the environment itself but what you allow into your camp. Protecting your resources—food, water, shelter—from predators or contamination is critical. Similarly, in leadership, you must defend your culture from negativity and toxic behaviors that threaten to derail progress.

In his book *The Energy Bus*, Jon Gordon warns about "energy vampires"—negative forces that can drain the life from your team.[22] As a leader, it's your responsibility to hold people accountable and prevent toxicity from entering and spreading in your culture.

Defending the line might involve difficult conversations to address behaviors that don't align with your culture. Much like setting boundaries to keep your camp safe, holding people accountable ensures the integrity of your culture and protects the relationships that nourish it.

Without a healthy culture rooted in positive relationships, any leadership strategy will wither. However, by intentionally nurturing these connections and creating a culture of belonging and excellence, you can build a team that thrives. Rock by rock, relationship by relationship—just like a carefully built shelter in the wilderness—you'll construct a cultural foundation that stands the test of time.

Apply What You've Learned

- ☐ **Workbook**: Go through this chapter's section in the Leadership on the Rocks workbook.
- ☐ **Relationship plan**: Decide what specific actions you will take to build positive relationships with others (one-on-ones, team building, celebrations, etc.).

- ☐ **Schedule your priorities**: Schedule the activities and actions you just defined in your relationship plan. (This can be for relationships at home too… Date night anyone?)
- ☐ **First impressions**: If you have any kind of opportunity to make a first impression on a person or group, plan out what you will do and say during that interaction.
- ☐ **Define the line**: Think about what you want your team, marriage, or family culture to be. Now define the culture you want to build by defining the beliefs, values, behaviors, common language, stories, traditions, and/or celebrations that you want to instill.
- ☐ **Coach the line**: Decide how you will model and teach the aspects of the culture created.
- ☐ **Defend the line**: Decide when and how you will give feedback to the individuals who are a part of the defined culture.

CHAPTER 7

Communication

Life-Giving Water

BEFORE I BECAME an administrator, I was an instructional coach. This position was unique because it allowed me to be involved in the school improvement planning process with administrators but also allowed me to partner with teachers to improve the quality of instruction within the classroom.

Each year as I sat in the room where initiatives were planned, I would take notes about all the details of the goals and key performance indicators (KPIs) and how it would all be implemented. After the initiatives were rolled out by administrators, I was then directly involved in supporting teachers to implement them.

For years I was able to observe how communication about the goals and expectations affected the relationship dynamics between the two groups. Being privy to the conversations happening on both sides of the school hallway, what I quickly saw was that the quality of communication directly impacted the quality of relationships and culture within that building.

This experience taught me a valuable lesson: Just as water sustains life, communication sustains relationships. I saw firsthand how strong, clear communication could nurture trust, foster collaboration, and invigorate a school's culture. On the other hand, when communication was muddled, inconsistent, or negative, relationships withered, leaving teams parched, directionless, and disengaged.

Water is life. In leadership, communication plays the same role. It flows through every interaction, carrying clarity, purpose, and understanding. Just as a stream nourishes the land it touches, effective communication nourishes relationships, ensuring they remain healthy and vibrant. Without it, misunderstandings take root like weeds, and relationships dry up, leaving a barren and unproductive culture.

This is why we must pack the water of effective communication in our Leadership on the Rocks survival kit. It quenches the thirst for connection and direction, ensuring your team is hydrated with the knowledge and purpose they need to move forward. Whether offering clear instructions, listening actively, or sharing feedback, communication keeps the flow of leadership smooth and sustainable.

If you aspire to succeed in leadership, packing and using the essential resource of communication is key. Without this vital provision, the heart of leadership—relationships—cannot thrive.

The Leadership on the Rocks Framework defines communication as the process of exchanging information from the sender to gain understanding and meaning from the receiver.

At its core, communication is about sharing information to gain knowledge and understanding, ultimately producing insight and wisdom. It acts as a steady stream that nourishes the heart of your team and serves as a litmus test for the health of your relationships and organizations.

Poor communication—or a complete lack thereof—leads to confusion, misinformation, frustration, and mistrust within an organization. It dries up the reservoirs of trust, leaving teams feeling disconnected and uncertain.

The good news, however, is that the opposite is also true. Effective communication fosters clarity, satisfaction, and trust, creating a thriving work environment. When leaders communicate well, it's like replenishing a dry field with refreshing rain, allowing relationships to bloom and organizations to flourish.

As a leader, a significant portion of your time will be devoted to communicating. You'll be building relationships, resolving conflicts, and delivering essential information. Communication is the water that keeps the heart of your leadership—relationships—alive and thriving.

It's imperative for leaders to be excellent communicators who can articulate the vision, mission, strategies, and tactics of their organization. However, being a great communicator extends beyond delivering clarity and inspiration; it also involves actively listening to and understanding others.

In *Leaders Eat Last*, Simon Sinek emphasizes the importance of leaders creating a "circle of safety" to protect their employees; this in turn "creates an environment for the free exchange of information and effective communication."[23] This "circle of safety" ensures that everyone in the organization feels nurtured and valued—a true hallmark of effective communication.

Communication is fundamentally about the exchange of information for meaning. To ensure your leadership stays hydrated and your relationships remain strong, let's explore three key communication goals:

- Knock out bad communication.
- Provide good communication.
- Get buy-in.

The heart of leadership revolves around valuing relationships, and positive relationships cannot flourish without effective communication. Where communication flows freely and effectively, relationships are strong, and the culture is vibrant. Where there is bad communication, there are bad relationships because the two are inseparably intertwined.

Knock Out Bad Communication

Before we can explore solutions for improving communication in our workplaces and homes, we must first identify the underlying problems. Poor communication is like contaminated water in your survival kit—it doesn't just fail to nourish; it actively harms. When the flow of communication is tainted, it seeps into relationships, eroding trust, clarity, and connection.

Understanding the behaviors that pollute communication is crucial for keeping our relationships healthy. While many factors contribute to bad communication, four key contaminants often poison the flow: selfishness, unspoken expectations, inappropriate formats, and distortion.

Selfishness

Because people naturally have a desire to be seen, heard, and valued, it is easy for communication to become self-focused. When individuals concentrate solely on their own needs to be acknowledged, they often overlook the importance of seeing, hearing, and valuing others.

When everyone communicates with the sole intent of expressing their own thoughts and feelings, understanding breaks down, resulting in a failure to communicate effectively.

This self-centeredness leads to a breakdown in the exchange that inevitably creates a failure to communicate.

Unspoken Expectations

Compounding the issue of bad communication is our tendency to have unspoken expectations. We assume that others understand our thoughts and desires without our voicing them.

Many people develop expectations internally but fail to communicate them externally to the relevant stakeholders. Leaders often express frustration, thinking "they should know." But they don't know because what you expected wasn't communicated. It's crucial to remember that people cannot read your mind! When leaders imply expectations without verbalizing them, they create confusion.

For example, a leader might think their employees should know how to prepare a report or give a great presentation though there has been no explicit communication or training on what that entails. The reality is that we often judge others on a game for which they weren't given the rules, and so they aren't sure how to play. This lack of clarity leads to frustration for all parties.

Format

The format of communication—how we convey our messages—can also lead to misunderstandings. Non-verbal cues, tone, and the context of communication significantly impact how messages are received. Bad formats include

- crossing your arms or turning away from the person you are communicating with,

- yelling louder or texting in all caps to drive your point home,
- starting a conversation about one problem but bringing up all the past grievances in the same conversation,
- having what should be a private conversation in front of others.

Yet when we communicate, we often do all four of these things, and none of them help the other person receive the message.

Unfortunately, we also have a tendency to say what's on our mind (to make us feel better) without any regard to whether or not it is the appropriate time or place.

Another huge grievance for format is when we "call people out" publicly. Adding public humiliation to the dynamic of the original problem is a *huge* offender to all relationships (from coworkers and employees to spouses and children). When you publicly embarrass or humiliate another person, you have done major damage to your relationship.

Distortion

Finally, distortion refers to how we fill in informational gaps with assumptions or narratives about others' intentions. When faced with uncertainty, our brains strive to make sense of the situation, often leading us to create false narratives. As described in the must-read book *Crucial Conversations*, a pattern of observing someone's behavior, forming a story (distortion) about their intent, and then feeling and reacting based on that story can result in miscommunication.[24]

Too often, the stories we tell ourselves about the other person are wrong, leading us to have the wrong response. Storytelling is one of the worst behaviors causing bad communication in our places of work and in our homes.

Now that we understand the roots of bad communication, we can work towards solutions. To enhance communication and foster better relationships, we should follow the four Cs of good communication.

The Four Cs of Communication

Just as water sustains and nourishes our bodies, effective communication fuels the heart of leadership and gives life to relationships. When communication flows clearly and freely, it replenishes trust, collaboration, and understanding. But like water, it must be drawn from a deep, reliable source.

As a leader, mastering the four Cs of communication—check your ego, clarity, channel, and converse—will allow you to nourish your relationships, strengthen your culture, and enhance your organization's effectiveness.

By incorporating these principles into your leadership, you will enhance your ability to listen, understand, and engage others meaningfully, fostering an environment of growth and cooperation. Without these key components, communication can become muddied and hinder progress, leading to frustration, miscommunication, and conflict.

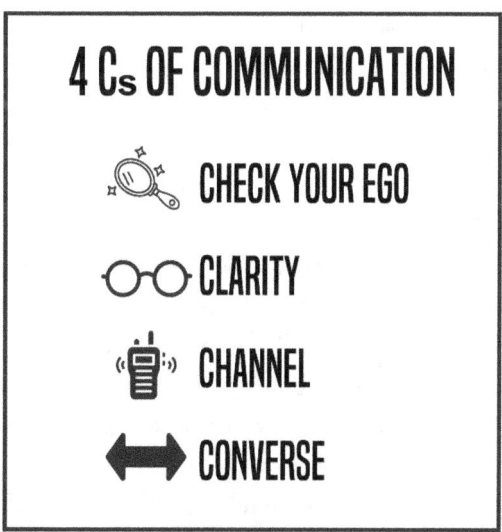

Check Your Ego

Ego often stands as a significant barrier to effective leadership. As leaders, we must remember that our primary role is to serve others, not to feed our own needs for affirmation, validation, or power.

Approach every interaction with the mindset "It's not about me; it's about you" or "We before me." This perspective shifts the focus away from self-interest and toward genuinely listening and understanding others.

My personal mantra that reminds me to check my ego and listen first to understand is the Bible verse James 1:19: "…let every person be *quick to hear*, *slow to speak*, slow to anger…" (emphasis added).

If we could all just follow this one guideline, imagine how much better our relationships would be at work and at home.

When engaging in conversations, don't listen merely to formulate your response. Stay curious about the thoughts, feelings, and circumstances of others. Ask open-ended questions and genuinely listen to what they are saying. This practice fosters trust and encourages a meaningful exchange of ideas.

Key Takeaway:

Clarity in communication can help you avoid a lot of problems.

Clarity

Clear communication helps avoid misunderstandings and fosters effective collaboration.

As a person who has worn glasses most of my life, I find that when I take them off, my vision becomes fuzzy. However, putting them back on restores clarity, enabling me to navigate confidently.

To communicate clearly is to provide others with the "glasses" they need to see their environment accurately. It's crucial to understand that people have different needs for clarity. Just as I can't hand you my glasses and expect you to see better, I can't assume everyone requires the same information to achieve clarity.

To provide clarity while considering these needs, develop a clear storyboard for your message. A storyboard refers to organizing your message into a logical sequence that is easily followed and understood like scenes from a movie would flow. You can create a storyboard by following these steps:

- *Clarify the big picture.* Create a concise key takeaway that summarizes the message.
- *Include story elements.* Identify the characters involved, the problem at hand, and the flow of the message.
- *Highlight main points.* Offer specific details about the what, who, when, how, and where.
- *Provide a "learn more" section.* Include an appendix, attachments, links to relevant articles, or opportunities for follow-up conversations.

By being intentional in providing clarity, you help others see the path ahead clearly.

Channel

Think back to childhood experiences with walkie-talkies. If you didn't have the right channel set, your message wouldn't come through; instead, you'd hear static. As a leader, you want to avoid static in your lines of communication.

Communication channels refer to how you convey your message, whether through conversation, meetings, presentations, or written communication. Selecting the wrong channel can lead to ineffective communication. For instance, some might host a meeting that could have been an email or send an email that should have been a conversation.

When deciding what channel to use, consider two critical factors: the audience receiving the message and the type of message being delivered. Is it informational? Directive? Does it require dialogue? Understanding the nature of your message is essential.

For example, an informational message can be conveyed through an email, while a directive often requires a conversation followed by an email. High-stakes or emotional messages should always be delivered face-to-face to avoid misunderstandings that often arise from written communication.

Attempting to resolve complex issues through email or text can lead to confusion, as recipients might interpret your words in unintended ways. Utilizing voice inflection and body language conveys sincerity, empathy, and understanding.

Another element that can cause static is distractions such as phone usage, sidebar conversations, or mental absence (e.g., thinking about another situation or daydreaming). The goal for communication is to have the message move through three phases among your audience: hearing it, understanding it, and taking action on it. Be sure to remove the distractions by requesting people's full attention.

Always choose the appropriate channel and remove distractions to ensure your message is received clearly.

Converse

To converse means to have a conversation. Engaging in a true exchange of ideas is vital for effective communication. This flow of information must be intentional, ensuring that conversation flows freely among all parties involved.

Avoid allowing one person—yourself included—to dominate the conversation. If this happens, the exchange becomes one-sided. Instead, focus on listening. Pastor and author Andy Stanley offers this warning: "Leaders who refuse to listen will eventually be surrounded by people who have nothing significant to say."[25]

To create an environment that encourages conversation, you may need to establish norms to guide the discussion. Here are some strategies to ensure a safe conversational environment:

- Establish clarity on the topics to be discussed and allow time for reflection.
- Set expectations to prevent domination of the speaking floor.
- Discourage distractions like cell phones during meetings.
- Ask open-ended questions to invite deeper discussion.
- Encourage engagement from those hesitant to speak up.
- Maintain open body language to foster a welcoming atmosphere.

As a leader, ensure that communication is not a one-way street. Reflect on your interactions, meetings, and conversations. Do you cultivate an environment where participants can converse freely? Do your employees feel empowered to share their ideas? If not, make a conscious effort to foster open dialogue.

Resolving Conflict

In leadership, conflict is inevitable. At times it feels like you're constantly navigating disputes, misunderstandings, and emotional storms. From physical altercations to fiery disagreements or the spread of misinformation, it can feel overwhelming. But just as water quenches thirst and cools a fever, effective communication is the refreshing antidote to conflict.

In my years of leadership, I've learned that the key to resolving and preventing conflict lies in how we communicate. Effective communication is key to resolving conflicts and preventing new issues from arising. Water has the ability to calm, cleanse, and restore harmony—and so does communication when it's used wisely. To positively impact relationships and move through conflict, you must be equipped to navigate difficult conversations with clarity and care. The right communication can de-escalate tensions, untangle misunderstandings, and allow relationships to flow smoothly again.

As you work to resolve conflicts, pay close attention to verbal and nonverbal cues between exchanges. Having the emotional intelligence to notice and interpret cues is like being your own meteorologist, capable of recognizing when a storm is brewing. This ability allows you to detect and address conflict as soon as it begins to emerge.

Those with the heart of leadership not only value people; they also know how to communicate with others in a way that resolves conflicts. *It is unresolved conflict that breeds bitterness and destroys relationships.*

The average leader spends significant time mediating conflict. By following the principles of effective communication—checking your ego, providing clarity, choosing the right channel, and fostering conversation—you dig the deep well of water necessary for healthy organizational culture to grow.

Getting Buy-in ROCKS

We've all heard the saying "You can lead a horse to water, but you can't make him drink." When it comes to leadership, this saying captures a key challenge: getting buy-in. No matter how great your ideas or strategies are, they can't succeed without the support and commitment of your team.

Think of buy-in as the mineral-rich water that helps your vision grow. Just as water is essential for life to thrive, clear proactive communication is vital to securing the support of your team. You can have all the resources in place, but if your team isn't "hydrated" with the right understanding and commitment, your efforts won't bear fruit. Effective communication ensures that everyone is aligned with the mission, understands their role, and is motivated to work together toward shared goals.

By focusing on communication strategies that build trust, clarity, and connection, you'll ensure your team not only drinks from the well of your vision but is ready to take action to achieve it.

You need buy-in to support the why, how, and what of the work to accomplish the goal.

Without this buy-in, your organization risks stagnation—sitting still in the ponds of the status quo to then become a breeding ground for harmful bacteria, viruses, and parasites.

Be warned, though: In leadership, *the* goal is not always *your* goal. Sometimes you may be handed a mandate that requires your team to deliver on an inflexible directive. When communicating complex or new information, obtaining buy-in is crucial to prevent interactions from going awry and damaging workplace relationships and culture.

Many organizational cultures experience extra conflict due to a lack of buy-in regarding leadership. Having a title that makes you "in charge" does not guarantee that your team will automatically support your vision or mission. You must be intentional about how you introduce new initiatives, deliver "big" news, or give presentations by focusing on your audience. Use the ROCKS method to plan your message and solidify buy-in.

The ROCKS method is a five-phase communication strategy that helps you plan your message effectively: relate it, organize it, communicate it, KISS it (keep it simple, stupid), and sustain it.

Relate It

The first step in the ROCKS method is to relate your message to the audience's current knowledge and feelings. By establishing a connection with where your audience is, you can bridge the gap in gaining buy-in.

Consider these questions as you prepare your message:

- What background information do they have?
- What do they not know but need to know?
- How does this message affect them individually?
- What feelings or questions can you anticipate they will have concerning the message?

Listeners always ask, "How does this affect me?" Proactively explain how your message relates to them. If various groups are affected differently, consider differentiating the dissemination of information. For instance, schedule separate meetings that share the same overarching theme but highlight the varying specifics of how each group is impacted. When your message resonates with the audience, it allows for better connection, engagement, and willingness to buy in.

Organize It

The second step is to organize your message to clarify why it matters, how it ties back to the bigger picture or mission, and what the audience needs to do in response.

Create a mantra (slogan or headline phrase) summarizing the entire concept, no matter how complex it may be. A well-crafted mantra simplifies the message and can serve as a rallying cry to maintain focus during times of change and chaos.

While concentrating on the *why* and *how* of your message, don't forget the *what*. Clearly outline what the audience needs to do in response to your message. Delivering information with no action point is usually a waste of time.

Communicate It

The third step involves determining how you will communicate your message. Your goal is for the audience to hear, understand, and take action based on your message. Build a communication plan that follows the four Cs of communication: Check your ego (make it about them), provide clarity, deliver through the right channel, and offer a way for people to converse about the message.

Always follow up after meetings or presentations with a recap email reiterating the *why*, *how*, and *what* of your message.

KISS It

The fourth step is to KISS it: Keep it simple, stupid. People don't read long emails/texts, and they struggle or refuse to follow long processes. Simplify your message and required actions to address only the essential information and steps.

If implementing a process, try to keep it to three to four steps, and create a one-page visual to simplify the message. A one-page summary serves as a powerful anchor chart, helping to solidify the message in people's minds.

In his book *Brief*, Joseph McCormack emphasizes that leaders must ensure their messages are clear, concise, and compelling.[26] He advocates for the one-page visual that tells a story.

Remember how teachers used to display posters explaining complex concepts? On test day, those posters would come down, but students could still visualize the information. This demonstrates the effectiveness of a one-page visual: It simplifies complex content into a memorable image, aiding understanding.

Sustain It

The fifth and final step is to sustain the message by focusing on three aspects: repeat, results, refine. Once the message or action is implemented, don't just set it and forget it.

Get comfortable with repeating your messages. The human brain takes time to absorb, interpret, and act on information, requiring about seven repetitions before something is learned. The higher your position in the organization, the more you'll have to repeat the message so it makes its way down to the individual contributor level.

Continue to repeat the message while analyzing for results. The results include the level of understanding, engagement, and acceptance of the message within the team. If the results show confusion, disengagement, or resistance then you need to refine the message.

Refining the message doesn't mean a complete overhaul or rewrite; it means making edits based on the audience feedback to better increase buy-in. Refining your message or actions based on the results of audience feedback allows for long-term sustainability.

Use the buy-in ROCKS method to plan your message rollout effectively.

COMMUNICATION

In our Leadership on the Rocks survival kit, relationships form the heart that keeps your leadership alive and thriving. But a heart, no matter how strong, can't function without proper hydration. That's where communication comes in—it's the water that flows through and sustains every connection.

When communication flows freely and effectively, your organization will transition from

- confusion to clarity,
- frustration to empathy,
- assumptions to trust.

Effective communication quenches the thirst for connection and direction. It ensures your team is hydrated with the knowledge and purpose they need to move forward. Whether it's offering clear instructions, listening actively, or sharing feedback, communication keeps your leadership flowing smoothly.

But waters of communication don't just sustain—pair them with the food of collaboration, and you bring people together not just for sustenance but for fellowship. Just as water nourishes the body, collaboration nourishes the spirit of your leadership. Let's explore how collaboration becomes the feast that nourishes and unifies your team.

Apply What You've Learned

☐ **Workbook**: Go through this chapter's section in the Leadership on the Rocks workbook.

- **Bad communication:** Reflect on any situations where you showcased the four aspects of bad communication: selfishness, unspoken expectations, format, and storytelling. How did it affect the relationship? What can you learn from that experience?
- **The four Cs of good communication:** Think about a conversation you need to have and plan out how you will communicate it using the four Cs.
  - Check your ego: How will you actively listen and stay focused on understanding the other person?
  - Clarity: How will you simplify and deliver your message so that the receiver can understand it? (Story elements? Main points? Providing access to more details?)
  - Channel: What format will you use to communicate with the other person?
  - Converse: How will you ensure there is dialogue between all parties (e.g., establish norms, discourage distractions, encourage engagement, employ non-verbal actions)?
- **Buy-in ROCKS method**: Think about a work project, presentation, or message you need to deliver. Plan that delivery using the ROCKS method below.
  - Relate it: Decide how you will relate the message to what your audience already knows and is currently feeling.
  - Organize it: Clarify why the message matters, how it ties back to the bigger picture or mission, and what the audience needs to do in response. Develop a mantra you can repeat to remind people of the message.
  - Communicate it: Create a communication plan using the four Cs of communication above so that the audience hears it, understands it, and can take action on it.
  - KISS it: Simplify the message or process and create a one-page visual for it.

COMMUNICATION

- ☐ Sustain it: Check for understanding and fidelity within the actions. Refine the message or work if needed.
- ☐ **One-page communication**: Think about a message, concept, or process your team struggles with. Create a one-page graphic to clarify the message and establish the essential key points or steps.

CHAPTER 8

Collaboration

The Food of Fellowship

WHEN I FIRST transitioned into a leadership role, I faced not only new responsibilities but also some of the most challenging times of my life, both professionally and personally. What kept me going during those tough years was the incredible collaboration of my team. My coworkers didn't just show up—they leaned in, offered support, and worked alongside me through each obstacle. Together, we overcame challenges, achieved great results, and created a culture that fueled our success.

That experience taught me a powerful lesson: Collaboration isn't just about getting work done; it's also the nourishment that sustains you in the toughest times. Just as we need food to maintain our energy, we need collaboration to keep our teams energized, aligned, and moving forward.

Once relationships are hydrated with clear communication, they need energy to grow and go. In the Leadership on the Rocks survival kit, collaboration is the food that fuels the heart of leadership.

Food does more than satisfy hunger—it brings people together. Around shared meals, stories are told, bonds are formed, and ideas are exchanged. Similarly, in leadership, collaboration fosters fellowship, teamwork, and connection. It nourishes the collective spirit of your team, allowing everyone to work together and create something greater than any one individual could achieve.

The Leadership on the Rocks Framework defines collaboration as the action of working with one or more people to produce or create something.

It's a simple concept, but getting people to communicate and work together will actually be one of the hardest things you do as a leader.

The unfortunate reality is that our work organizations usually put a bunch of employees in the same room and tell them to "go forth and create results." But this only creates a group of people. It doesn't produce a team, and it definitely doesn't ensure that collaboration occurs among everyone.

Without true collaboration, relationships stagnate, and the heart of leadership weakens. Leaders must provide the right "meal plan" to ensure their teams are energized and aligned—creating opportunities for meaningful teamwork, fostering trust and mutual respect, and celebrating collective wins.

When leaders prioritize collaboration, they build an environment where everyone has a seat at the table. This shared experience doesn't just sustain; it strengthens and unites, transforming teams into thriving communities.

Collaboration is more than just dividing tasks; it's about bringing together diverse perspectives, skills, and ideas to create something greater than what any individual could achieve alone. It's the act of sharing, supporting, and working together toward a common goal. When collaboration is present, it unites people and drives progress. Without it, teams can become fragmented, uninspired, and stagnant.

As you pack collaboration into your Leadership on the Rocks survival kit, remember that it's more than a tool for getting things done—it's the essential fuel that powers your leadership. In this chapter, we'll explore how to cultivate a collaborative environment where diverse perspectives are valued, everyone is engaged, and the collective strength of your team drives success.

Harnessing the Power of Diverse Perspectives

During the COVID-19 quarantine, my spouse and I would take daily walks through our wooded neighborhood park. He's nine inches taller than me, so I struggled to keep up with his stride. One day, while I was focused on keeping pace, he nudged me to the side of the path just as a bicycle zipped past us. I hadn't noticed it at all. Later, I saved him from stepping on a disgusting half-eaten mouse in our path, only to realize he hadn't noticed that either.

We laughed at how our differing perspectives aligned with our personalities. He's a planner, always thinking ahead, while I'm more present focused, enjoying the moment. He sees the forest, and I see the tree in front of me.

This walk reminded me of the value of diverse perspectives. In leadership and teamwork, differing viewpoints, skills, and personalities are assets, not obstacles. When we collaborate and appreciate each other's unique strengths, we not only gain a fuller view of the path ahead, but we also build stronger, more effective teams. Just as a survivalist needs a well-rounded tool kit—a compass for direction, a map for understanding the terrain, and tools for building shelter—successful teams need a mix of perspectives and skills to navigate challenges and reach their goals.

Leaders who want teams to collaborate know that they need diversity of thought, skills, perspectives, and personalities. If a team is filled with people who are all alike, there will be major gaps in skills and blind spots that weaken the work.

Therefore, every team needs diversity amongst its members to be fully equipped for the best performance possible. It's the variety of and differences in people that make relationships and teams so exciting and enriching, but these also create an added layer of complexity.

No matter the varying levels of diversity, dynamics, and complexity that relationships and teams have, or the difficulties and conflicts that can come with them, every person adds value. This is the power of diversity and collaboration.

In your leadership, you need to know not only your own strengths and constraints but those of your team as well. Then find people who compliment and complete those qualities and skill sets. Remembering your team's strengths and constraints is especially important when hiring a new team member. Know the skill and knowledge gap your team has and look for candidates who can bring that skill or knowledge to the team.

If you want your team to collaborate, then it is your job as the leader to make it a priority. Too many managers call a group of people a team yet don't build a culture of teamwork and collaboration. This is a huge mistake. Once you've put together a group of diverse people, it's your job to ensure they become a team that knows how to collaborate.

However, before we get to the action of building collaborative teams, we have to start with understanding yet another layer of the psychology behind people, this time focused on group behaviors.

The Psychology Behind Teams: Nourishing the Mind and Spirit

Just as food nourishes our bodies, the psychology behind a team's dynamics determines how that nourishment is consumed and converted into energy. Throughout the head, heart, hands, and guts of leadership, the internal thoughts and feelings of each individual directly impact the external interactions and collaboration within the team. Understanding these psychological elements is crucial because they can either fuel or hinder a team's success.

In today's work culture, teams are central to our way of achieving results. And just like a balanced meal, effective collaboration requires careful consideration of each person's internal drivers—emotions, thoughts, and personal perspectives. These elements come together to create a well-functioning, thriving team.

Collaboration is not just important; it's the essential ingredient that binds everything together.

There are three nourishing resources I recommend when it comes to growing your understanding of the psychology behind forming collaborative teams. First is the DISC Personality Indicator, an assessment tool that measures four aspects of a person's personality: dominance (D), influence (I), steadiness (S), and conscientiousness (C).[27] This assessment provides tremendous insight into areas such as motivation, ideal environment, communication, strengths, and more. (If you want to learn more about your team members, consider using the DISC personality assessment. You can learn more about it at www.leadershipontherocks.com.)

The second resource is Tuckman's Stages of Group Development—forming, storming, norming, performing, and adjourning—that explains the natural progressions and universal principles behind team development.[28] The third resource is Patrick Lencioni's book *The 5 Dysfunctions of a Team*—dealing with trust, conflict, commitment, accountability, and results—that shares the most universal yet basic dysfunctions of all teams.[29]

I have found *great* success in teaching these principle-based concepts to all my teams because they create awareness of the psychology at play behind working with others.

I encourage you to teach these concepts (or other psychology or personality theories) to your teams to increase their awareness of and empathy for the psychology behind relationship and team building. It will only accelerate the team's success in collaboration because they will develop the psychological understanding and soft skills needed to build a positive team culture.

When it comes to teams, I must also give you a warning here: Watch for competition among your team culture. While competition can be healthy (in that it can motivate people to grow their skills), what typically happens in the workplace is unhealthy competition, namely, competition of status.

It is human nature for people to want status that can come in the form of power, money, fame, title, or access. This can also mean that for people to increase their own status they must work to decrease someone else's status.

This is junior high and high school lunch-table-status wars all over again where people try to blow out another's proverbial candle to make their own shine brighter.

As you work to build your collaborative team, you need to pay close attention to how team members are interacting. As the status of each person on the team changes for good or bad, their trust of and within the team changes for good or bad.

Team Building

Just like a family meal, team building can either be something that's eagerly anticipated or met with eye rolls and cynicism. Just as the right ingredients can transform a simple meal into a nourishing feast, the way you approach team building can create an environment of trust, empathy, and collaboration—or leave your team feeling unfulfilled. Most leaders know that team building is essential, but it's the approach they take that determines whether their efforts will truly nourish the team.

So what's the key ingredient that will determine how your team internalizes this process? The answer is *authenticity* in relationship building.

Authenticity, like the freshest ingredients, is key to fostering an environment where people feel safe to be themselves and where trust can flourish. Just as a meal's flavor depends on the quality of the ingredients, a team's success depends on how genuine and real the interactions are.

Team building isn't a one-time event; it's nourished over time through everyday interactions. When people do the following, they create the kind of environment where trust and collaboration thrive:

- encourage each other in tough moments
- challenge one another to grow
- work to resolve conflict
- speak to one another with respect
- support each other through challenges
- serve or assist one another in their tasks

It's the pattern of these daily interactions—small acts of kindness, communication, and support—that will cement whether your team feels like a cohesive unit or simply a group forced together. When leaders cultivate a space for authentic, meaningful interactions, they lay the foundation for collaboration to flourish. Like a slow-cooked meal, the right ingredients and time make all the difference.

Three Phases of Building a Collaborative Team

Everyone wants to be part of a winning team, but a silent killer of success for most teams is a lack of true collaboration. Just like a meal can't nourish the body without the right balance of ingredients, a team can't succeed without intentional collaboration between its members.

Unlike playground teams in childhood, where we often choose our teammates, we don't always get to select the people on our professional teams. Instead, people are sometimes placed on teams together by necessity, and where there are diverse individuals, there will inevitably be conflict. When relationships are forced or not nurtured, gaps in communication widen, creating even greater tensions.

Establishing a team does not automatically guarantee effective collaboration. It requires intentional action from both the leader and the members themselves.

Let's dig into the three essential phases for building a collaborative team. Each phase is like a key step in preparing a nourishing meal that will fuel a high-performing team, sustaining them through the challenges they face.

Key Takeaway:

Collaboration doesn't just happen; it must be cultivated and coached.

3 PHASES OF BUILDING A COLLABORATIVE TEAM

 **PURPOSE**

 **PARAMETERS**

 **COACHING**

 **BONUS: INTEGRATION**

Phase 1: Purpose

The first phase in building a collaborative team is clearly communicating the purpose and vision. Without a shared understanding of why they're working together, teams can quickly lose their sense of direction, just like a meal without a clear recipe or a team without a common cause.

Before jumping into the tasks, it's crucial that you clearly communicate the *why* behind the team's formation and the vision for where their work will take them. People need to rally around a common cause—a shared purpose that unites them. When everyone understands the ultimate goal, they can move forward together, fueling each other's efforts along the way.

Here are some questions to answer when defining the purpose behind creating the team:

- What is the ultimate goal of the team? (Be specific.)
- What are they working toward?

- Are they improving efficiency, solving a problem, or developing a new product?
- Why are these specific people on the team? What unique skills do they bring?
- How will the work the team is doing contribute to a larger mission?

Communicating this purpose clearly and consistently will provide the nutritional foundation for collaboration. It's like providing the right fuel for the work ahead.

Phase 2: Parameters

Once the purpose is established, the next phase is to provide the team with clear parameters. Parameters act like the boundaries and guidelines that help ensure everyone works together cohesively, just like ingredients that must be carefully measured to create a balanced meal.

Without knowing the expectations, team members can feel like they're working blindly, unsure of what they should be doing or where they stand. Parameters clarify what needs to be done, how to approach the work, and what success looks like. They set a framework within which the team can collaborate efficiently and effectively.

These are some key parameters:

- Must-dos and should-dos (mandatory requirements and best practices)
- Defined team roles and responsibilities
- Behavioral norms and expectations
- Deadlines and milestones
- Communication guidelines (e.g., up, down, and across the organization)

- Available resources and tools (to store, support, and add value to the work)

The clearer the parameters, the easier it will be for the team to collaborate effectively and keep the work moving forward without unnecessary confusion.

One effective tool for fostering collaboration is the RACI chart to clarify roles and responsibilities:

- Responsible—who completes the task?
- Accountable—who oversees and approves the work?
- Consulted—who provides input on the task?
- Informed—who needs updates on the task or project?

Pair the RACI chart with a "living" digital document to centralize project information, clarifications, and collaboration. This reduces the need for endless email chains and keeps everyone aligned.

Phase 3: Coaching

Just as food requires careful attention and timing to turn out well, teams need ongoing coaching to stay on track and improve. Leadership doesn't end after establishing purpose and parameters; continuous coaching is key to ensuring the team is working cohesively and moving toward success.

Leaders must be present, actively engaging with the team and providing timely feedback. Coaching isn't about taking over the work but about guiding the team through challenges, offering constructive guidance, and reinforcing positive progress. This feedback loop is critical—it's like the last step of preparing a meal, where you check the seasoning, adjust the flavors, and ensure everything is balanced before serving it.

Effective coaching involves

- offering consistent and timely feedback,
- celebrating successes to boost morale,
- encouraging open communication and feedback within the team, and
- addressing issues or concerns as they arise to keep things on course.

When leaders provide the necessary support and guidance, teams are better equipped to overcome obstacles and stay focused on their shared goal.

Bonus Phase 4: Integration of Teams

For teams ready to level up, there's an advanced phase: the integration of teams across departments, functions, or even organizations. This bonus phase is like creating a multicourse meal, where the components of the team must blend together seamlessly to achieve a common goal.

COLLABORATION

Cross-functional teams often face the challenge of aligning diverse skills, perspectives, and goals. But when done right, the integration of teams can spark innovation and drive performance at new levels. However, integration can be a complex and delicate process, and without a solid foundation in the earlier phases, it can easily fall apart.

To succeed, you'll need to coach your teams through the integration process, helping them build trust, align their efforts, and communicate effectively across boundaries. Leaders who foster this level of collaboration create a stronger, more unified organization capable of tackling the toughest challenges.

As we wrap up our deep dive into collaboration, it's clear that in today's world of work, teamwork is no longer optional—it's essential. As leaders, we must be intentional about how we build our teams, ensuring that collaboration is a key ingredient in the leadership mix. In fact, fostering a collaborative environment is essential for success. Teams that fail to collaborate effectively will only produce confusion, conflict, and work that's misaligned, undermining the goals they set out to achieve.

Your Leadership on the Rocks survival kit must have the essentials to provide the energy for your leadership body. When it comes to nourishing and protecting the heart of leadership—relationships—the provisions of communication and collaboration form the foundation of your leadership survival kit.

These provisions sustain you to not just survive but thrive. They will help you build a leadership culture where teams are nourished, supported, and motivated, and where your own leadership journey continues to grow stronger. When these elements are in place, they create a culture that is healthy, vibrant, and capable of overcoming the challenges we inevitably face.

By prioritizing relationships, communication, and collaboration, you're setting yourself and your teams up for long-term success. Together, these elements will ensure that your leadership remains as strong and resilient as the rocks you've built it on.

Apply What You've Learned

- ☐ **Workbook**: Go through this chapter's section in the Leadership on the Rocks workbook.
- ☐ **Diversity of skills**: Analyze your team's strengths and constraints. Decide what skills and perspectives are missing and hire for them.
- ☐ **Team building:** Decide what specific actions you will take to foster connection and build positive relationships among those on the team (meals, personality assessments with follow up activities, community service projects, etc.).
- ☐ **Professional development**: Decide what personal and professional development training you will provide for your team (psychology theories, personality assessments, team development phases, leadership development, etc.).
- ☐ **Schedule your priorities**: Schedule the team-building and professional development activities.
- ☐ **Three phases of building collaborative teams:** Be intentional in creating collaborative teams by communicating purpose, providing parameters, and coaching for success.

COLLABORATION

- ☐ Purpose: What is the ultimate goal of the team? (Be specific.) What skills does each team member bring to the table?
- ☐ Parameters: Define the parameters for the work or assign the team to define them (must-dos, should-dos, norms, roles, jargon, deadlines, resources, requirements, location of the work, communication up/down/across the organization)
- ☐ Coaching: Decide when and how feedback will be given/received to add quality and value to the product or team.
- ☐ Bonus phase of integration: If the team is ready for integration, decide what problem the integrated team needs to solve. Looking across the organization, decide who needs to be added to the team because they can add value and insight.

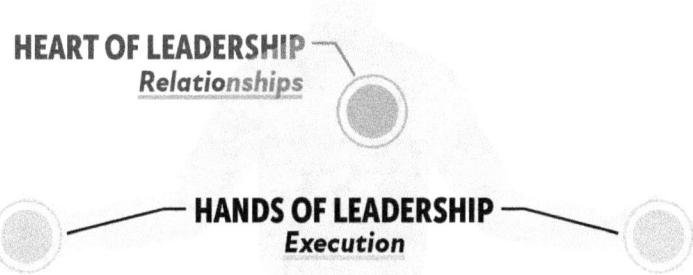

HEART OF LEADERSHIP
Relationships

Mindset

HANDS OF LEADERSHIP
Execution

PART 4

The Hands of Leadership

Creating Tools to Overcome Challenges

CHAPTER 9

Execution

The Multiuse Tools

BEFORE STEPPING INTO leadership, I considered myself a people-pleasing high achiever. I thrived on the satisfaction of being busy and the rush of checking tasks off my to-do list. But as I quickly discovered, leadership wasn't about how much I *did*; it was about how effectively I directed my energy toward what truly mattered.

In the early days of my leadership journey, I was overwhelmed by the sheer number of people and tasks vying for my attention. I was constantly pulled in multiple directions, trying to please everyone while simultaneously tackling an ever-growing list of responsibilities.

Despite working tirelessly, I always felt blocked or sidetracked—like my efforts weren't translating into real progress.

The turning point came during a particularly chaotic period when I realized that my busyness wasn't the same as productivity. I was pouring my energy into the wrong places. I was investing in relationships that nourished my *heart* of leadership, but my *hands*—the part of me responsible for action—were ill-equipped, missing the tools I needed to execute effectively.

That's when I learned an essential truth: Survival in leadership depends on more than just connection and vision. It requires the ability to act decisively and resourcefully. I needed to pack my survival kit with the right tools to cut through distractions, eliminate inefficiencies, and focus on actions that truly mattered.

Execution is the cornerstone of leadership survival. The hands of leadership are your builders and problem-solvers, equipping you with the mechanisms to transform plans into progress.

Execution functions like the ultimate multi-tool in your survival kit. Just as a Swiss Army Knife® or Leatherman® enables you to handle diverse challenges in the wilderness, the ability to execute empowers you to adapt, innovate, and overcome obstacles efficiently and effectively. It's what transforms vision into results and strategy into success.

But here's the thing: Time is not just money—it's life. How you spend your time as a leader not only shapes your results but also impacts the experience and well-being of your team. Wasting time on unnecessary tasks or inefficient processes drains energy, forces employees to extend their workdays into personal time, and stalls progress.

The truth is many leaders fall into the trap of looking busy rather than being productive. This focus on activity over outcomes keeps their teams stuck in a cycle of inefficiency that never moves the needle. As a leader, you must focus your time and energy on what is *mission critical*.

At the end of the day, your role as a leader is to build a better organization. That means executing a plan that grows results, increases productivity, boosts morale, and expands your organization's influence and impact.

In part 2 of *Leadership on the Rocks*, we focused on surviving the mental game by building a stronger self—equipping the head of leadership (mindset) with tools like the compass of identity and the map of purpose. In part 3, we cultivated the heart of leadership (relationships) by nourishing a healthy working culture through the waters of communication and food of collaboration.

In this chapter, we turn to the hands of leadership. With a strong mind and a connected heart, you've created the momentum needed to build a team that delivers real results. It's time to roll up your sleeves, pick up your tools, and start building a thriving, results-driven organization through execution.

Knowing What Is Mission Critical

When people think of execution, they often equate it with simply "getting things done." But busyness doesn't equal productivity, and even productivity doesn't guarantee meaningful results. *Execution is not about checking tasks off a list; it's about carrying out a proactive plan that ensures the right tasks are accomplished.*

Unfortunately, many workplaces fall into the trap of mistaking activity for progress. Employees spend their days buried under a pile of red tape, pet projects, or pointless meetings, chopping down trees in the wrong

Key Takeaway:

Execution isn't just activity—it's intentionality. To execute effectively, focus your time and energy on what's mission critical.

forest. Have you ever found yourself thinking, *Why am I doing this? It's such a waste of time!* That frustration stems from a lack of clarity and focus—something that only strong leadership can provide.

Think of execution as a multiuse tool in your leadership survival kit. Like a Swiss Army Knife®, it's versatile and powerful but only if used with precision. It's not about wildly hacking at every obstacle; it's about strategically choosing the tool that will best cut through distractions and carve a path forward.

I've often heard the analogy that true leaders don't just charge forward with their teams, chopping down trees as they go. Instead, they climb to the top of the tallest tree to ensure they're even in the right forest. As leaders, we must do the same—ensuring our teams are focused on the vital few rather than the trivial many.

Greg McKeown captures this principle beautifully in *Essentialism*, explaining how people feel most frustrated when their work is scattered across the trivial many but most fulfilled when they focus on the vital few.[30] Leaders must act as the filters for their teams, cutting through the noise to identify and communicate what's truly mission critical.

When leaders are clear about priorities, their teams feel empowered to say no to distractions and yes to the work that drives results. A laser-focused team, united around what matters most, is an unstoppable force.

By focusing your time and energy on what's mission critical, you'll wield your multiuse tool of execution with skill and precision, creating momentum that propels your team toward meaningful progress and success.

The Urgent/Important Matrix: Prioritizing Your Energy

Before Dwight D. Eisenhower became president in 1953, he served as supreme commander of the Allied Expeditionary Force during

EXECUTION

World War II. Describing his workload as overwhelming doesn't even begin to capture the full extent of it. But as an effective leader, Eisenhower understood the importance of focus. He knew he couldn't "do it all," so he developed a way to prioritize his time and energy based on what was urgent and important. This method became known as the Urgent/Important Matrix, a tool that remains invaluable for leaders today.

Just as Eisenhower used this tool to prioritize amidst the chaos of war, leaders today can use it as an apparatus in the multiuse tool of execution to manage their time and energy efficiently. Think of this matrix as sharpening your vision and focus, ensuring your hands of leadership are cutting through the right tasks, not just drowning in busywork.

You may not be leading an army or a country, but your leadership effectiveness hinges on how well you prioritize. The Urgent/Important Matrix helps you categorize tasks, ensuring your efforts align with mission-critical goals. Here's how to use it with your ever-growing to-do list:

- *Do* the tasks that are both important and urgent.
- *Schedule* the tasks that are important but not urgent.
- *Delegate* the tasks that are urgent but not important.
- *Don't do*, or eliminate, the tasks that are neither important nor urgent.

Using this matrix allows leaders to invest their energy wisely, focusing not only on immediate needs but also on actions that support long-term vision and impact. When you wield this tool, you free your hands of leadership to work smarter, not harder, and direct your team with clarity and purpose.

By pausing to ask if a task is truly worthy of your attention, you avoid the pitfall of reacting to every demand. This approach keeps you grounded, reduces stress, and positions your team to make meaningful progress.

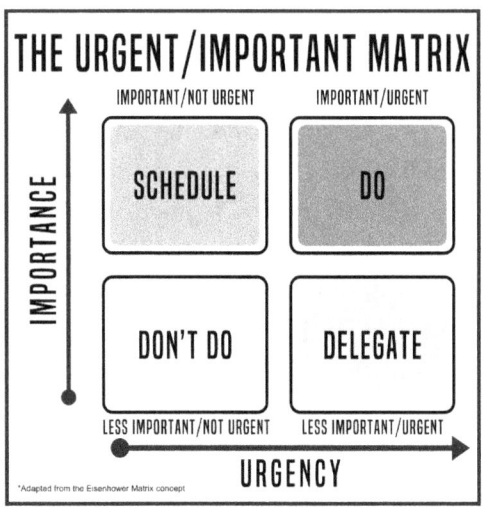

Proactive Plans: Those Who Fail to Plan, Plan to Fail

Have you ever heard nutritionists advise meal planning to avoid unhealthy temptations? They often say, "Those who fail to plan, plan to fail." Leadership operates much the same way. Without a proactive plan, the hands of leadership risk fumbling through chaos rather than building a clear path forward.

Leaders who know and do what is most mission critical, always have and carry out a short-term (goal), long-term (mission), and/or contingency (crisis) plan that is proactive. While many leaders might claim to have a plan, there's a crucial distinction between having a plan and executing a proactive one. Proactive plans aren't just ideas on paper—they're the structured actions that your multiuse tool enables you to carry out effectively.

EXECUTION

Why do plans fail in execution?

- Problems arise from chaos that stems from a lack of structure.
- Conflicts are born from miscommunication or unclear expectations.
- Constraints result from limited time, resources, or expertise.

Add to this the tendency to waste time on non-mission-critical tasks, and you've got a dull, ineffective tool. Execution sharpens this tool, creating structure, clarity, and efficiency to mitigate these common challenges.

Essential leaders use their multiuse tool of execution with precision by focusing on three core attributes:

- They are *proactive*. They anticipate obstacles, communicate clearly, and act with foresight.
- They are *people focused*. They prepare their teams for challenges, providing the communication and reassurance needed to navigate uncertainty.
- They are *intentional*. They ensure their teams have clarity, structure, and resources, enabling them to succeed in any environment.

The best leaders can always answer three critical questions:

1. Where do we need to go?
2. How will we get there?
3. How will we measure success?

So make sure to equip your hands of leadership with this essential apparatus of execution, guiding your team toward results that matter.

The Four Principles Behind a Plan of Action

Every leader needs to build and execute a proactive plan to fix the chaos that creeps up on the team. Whether facing a typical Monday morning or a surprise Jumanji-level crisis, a well-crafted plan equips your team to work through uncertainty and stay on course toward mission-critical goals.

Leaders don't react; they respond. Nobody wants a leader using the blunt edge of their leadership tool, hacking away at problems with emotional, knee-jerk decisions born of anger, fear, or anxiety. Instead, great leaders sharpen their focus, wielding their tools with precision to analyze and address challenges effectively. (I hope some executives read this paragraph.)

They need to analyze the situation through the four principles behind a plan of action:

1. Assess the situation first. Unless safety is being threatened, you have time to think through a situation before acting. Just as a survivalist checks the landscape for obstacles and opportunities, leaders need to uncover the facts, identify root causes, and focus on one problem or opportunity at a time. Most issues stem from gaps in safety, communication, organization, resources, skills, or motivation. When you peel back the layers, you'll find the true challenge your tool must address.
2. Establish structure to reduce chaos. To reduce chaos, equip your team with the right tools: define the end goal (the purpose of the tool), create systems (the mechanics of how it works), and establish processes (the tasks it will perform). With a clear structure, leaders give their teams the grip they need to tackle gaps and make meaningful progress.

3. **Provide clear communication.** Share how the plan assists the team. People always want to know what's happening and how it affects them. Be able to answer these questions: What's going on? How does this affect "me"? Why should I buy in? Leaders must communicate clearly and proactively to reduce confusion and keep everyone aligned. This is why communication plans like the ROCKS method are so helpful in guiding all leadership messages.
4. **Synthesize, summarize, and sustain your plan.** Once your plan is in place, keep it sharp. Package the plan neatly, highlight its main points, and provide ongoing support to ensure it remains effective. Just as a tool loses its edge without maintenance, a plan falls apart without follow-through. Leaders who consistently support their plans build trust and ensure their team has the clarity and resources to succeed. Always deliver your plan in a way your team can hear it, see it, understand it, and implement it.

No matter what plan you need to build for your role, follow these four principles to ensure your tool of execution is effective (achieving results) and efficient (minimizing resistance).

The One-Page Plan

For those needing extra directions on how to use a plan as a tool, don't worry. Plans are your strategy for getting the work done and are tailored to the goal, mission, or situation, but they don't have to be complex or require a ton of preparation, red tape, or paperwork. *It's more about the intentional thinking before acting than anything else.* The following are generic instructions for creating a one-page plan as a tool to execute and get results.

THE ONE-PAGE PLAN

0 Build positive relationships

1 Identify strategic priority and goal

2 Define challenges (gaps to overcome)

3 Desired outcomes and key partners

4 Choose approach (strategy)

5 Align strategy to key tenets

6 Generate tactics and timelines

7 Roll out using buy-in ROCKS

8 Build momentum

9 Create appendix (learn more section)

Step 0: Build positive relationships.

Reflective question: Do I have positive relationships with the stakeholders this plan will affect?

Even as we get into the details of creating a proactive plan, the culture of your team will always influence its effectiveness. No matter what aspect of leadership we're discussing, the psychology behind people and relationships is integral to leadership work.

Step 1: Identify the strategic priority and goal.

Reflective question: What is the one thing that will make the greatest positive impact given the current situation?

When creating your first plan, ask, "What is the most mission-critical issue that needs to be addressed right now?" Choose one priority to design a plan around. Determine if the plan is for

- short-term goals (to be accomplished within a year),
- long-term goals (the mission for your team), or
- contingency (e.g., emergency).

Align your plan with company goals and policies and industry best practices.

Step 2: Define challenges.

Reflective question: What obstacles could get in the way of accomplishing our goal?

Identify challenges that you and your team need to remove, address, or overcome. Conduct a SWOT analysis (strengths, weaknesses, opportunities, and threats) to identify internal and external challenges. External challenges are usually market or industry driven. Internal challenges can be budget, skills, or relational gaps to overcome. Start by assessing yourself first (since upper leadership is often the bottleneck) and then move to your team.

Step 3: Pinpoint desired outcomes and key partners.

Reflective questions: What does success really look like? How will we know if we are winning? Who can help us win?

Determine desired outcomes (what "good" looks like) and define your metrics for success (e.g., key performance indicators or KPIs). Think of KPIs as a scoreboard for a game—how will your team know if they're winning or losing? Ask, "Who else in the organization can help us win?" Partnering with support teams like HR, finance, or technology can expedite progress and reduce roadblocks.

Step 4: Choose an approach (strategy).
Reflective question: What is the one thing we will *do* to achieve our goal?

In step 4, decide your actual strategy (big picture *how*) to accomplish your goal. Gather input from your team and key partners, keeping the strategy simple to ensure implementation. Strategies that are too complex often die out due to confusion.

Step 5: Align strategy to key tenets (principles addressed).
Reflective question: How does our strategy align with core values and leadership or industry principles?

Every strategy should be built on key tenets explaining the *why* behind it. Each strategy usually has a people, process, and product element, so clearly state which tenet anchors these. Develop simple mantras and visuals that remind everyone of the plan and the bigger picture.

Step 6: Generate tactics and timelines.
Reflective questions: What day-to-day procedures will we implement to accomplish our *how* and *why*? When does each phase need to be completed and measured for progress?

Your strategy needs specific tactics (day-to-day *what*) defined. Empower your team to take the lead in defining methods that can be implemented daily to accomplish the goal. Define timelines and chunk your plan into phases so you can gauge progress along the way.

Warning: Nothing is more costly to a company's budget and organizational health than zigzagging between various strategies. I caution leaders against pushing all of your "strategy poker chips" in on one tactic. A well-thought-out strategy (e.g., better communication, saving money, transformation) can have a myriad of tactics (software systems, team training programs, workflow automation tools) that can be implemented within it.

Step 7: Roll out using buy-in ROCKS method.
Reflective question: What is the message for the plan (storyboard), and how will I get people to buy in?

How you roll out your plan to stakeholders matters a lot. If you don't connect with them initially, implementing the plan becomes an uphill battle. Save yourself time and resources by proactively packaging a rollout plan using a buy-in strategy like the ROCKS method.

Step 8: Build momentum.
Reflective question: How can we celebrate quick wins to build momentum?

In *Good to Great*, Jim Collins emphasizes that no one action will create dramatic transformation. It's the steady push on a heavy flywheel that creates momentum.[31] Celebrate early wins to gain momentum. Sustained communication about progress will keep the team moving toward the goal.

Step 9: Create an appendix (learn more).
Reflective question: How can I organize information so that others can access it if needed?

Organize resources (reports, policies, how-tos, budgets, timelines, etc.) in an appendix for your team and stakeholders to reference. This final step will enable your hard work to make a difference in the future.

These nine generic steps for creating a proactive plan are like adding attachments to your multiuse survival tool; each one enhances your ability to tackle any leadership challenge or seize new opportunities. Just as tools need regular use and maintenance to remain effective, this planning cycle should be repeated as you analyze results, sharpen your strategies, and learn from each executed plan. Over time, your leadership tool kit will become more refined, empowering you to navigate even the toughest terrain with confidence and precision.

New Leader Transition Plan

Transitioning into a new role can feel like setting out on an uncharted expedition. Without a clear map or the right tools, it's easy to get lost. But leadership success, like survival in the wilderness, isn't left to chance—it's built on preparation, strategy, and intentional action. That's why having a new leader transition plan is essential.

Think of this plan as equipping you with the tools and mindset to chart your course, empower your team, and make a lasting impact. By breaking your transition into three critical phases—equip, empower, and impact—you can ensure you're prepared to meet challenges head-on and build momentum toward long-term success.

Equip: The Learning Phase

The first month requires internal (self-focused) and external (organization-focused) transitions. The goal is to get equipped by identifying and utilizing the most essential information, skills, and tools needed for success. There are four ways to find your footing in the first month:

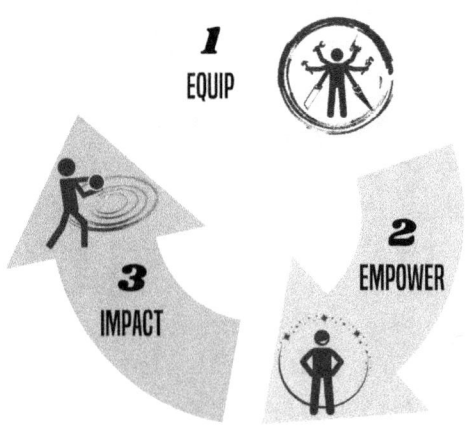

- *Develop a leader mindset.* Anchor yourself before challenges arise by cultivating a leader mindset and defining your key tenets. By reminding yourself of your identity, stating your purpose, and reframing statements and mantras, what you're really doing is anchoring yourself before the storms come.
- *Broaden your perspective.* Prepare to see a bigger picture. Your horizon needs to broaden to encompass a wider set of diversity, cultures, issues, and decisions. Ask yourself how an individual decision can/will scale positively or negatively across the team and organization.
- *Make a great first impression.* Create positive first impressions when meeting new people and tackling initial problems. Once people form an opinion about your effectiveness, it can be difficult to shift their perspective.
- *Advance your learning.* Research, read, and ask questions to accelerate your understanding of leadership, the organization, and your team. You're not magically going to be wiser or have more leadership skills the day after your promotion is announced.

Empower: The Action Phase

In your second month, focus on becoming fully immersed in the team. You want to know the team, understand the work, and find the obstacles and gaps that hinder team wins. By gaining clarity of your purpose, you develop urgency to act. Here are some ways to make those things happen:

- *Build positive relationships.* Concentrate on building trust and rapport with the team and stakeholders. People only want to work with people they know, like, trust, and respect.
- *Assess internal and external challenges.* Identify the challenges (e.g., what's hindering work or team culture) and assess their

root causes. You don't have to solve them all now but do identify them.
- *Identify desired outcomes and key partners.* Categorize desired outcomes and identify key partners to help reach them. When you are in a new role, your administrative assistant, as well as your finance and HR departments should be your best friends as you "learn the ropes."
- *Prioritize goals and strategize your approach.* Prioritize the most critical goals and begin developing a strategy for your top desired outcome. Use your personal mantras so you don't freak out at "all the things" that need to be addressed. (My favorite mantras are "I don't have to know all the answers or fix all the problems right now." "The best way to eat an elephant is one bite at a time.")

Impact: The Results Phase

Around your third month, you may be ready to begin executing goals to become a catalyst for positive change. However, learn to read the situation to ensure the team is ready. Don't start throwing out mandates on day sixty-two just because you're in your third month. There are four strategies to come through this period with success:

- *Build momentum through quick wins.* Look for "low-hanging fruit" or minor problems you can eliminate to build momentum. Whatever you do, don't add work to the team's plate. Think about what you can eliminate or automate to get the quick win.
- *Get buy-in for your vision and next steps.* Cast a vision of what success looks like and explain the *why* behind the *what*. People's behaviors don't change until their beliefs change so always point to the bigger purpose.

- *Execute, assess, refine, sustain (EARS)*. Don't set it and forget it with your plan but keep your "EARS" to the ground. Continually assess and refine the blueprint to ensure its sustainability.
- *Structure for expansion*. Never rest on your laurels. Continue building a foundation for future growth and start the cycle over again. Keep thinking ahead about the next step towards improvement and then start the equip, empower, impact cycle all over again.

Just as a seasoned adventurer revisits their tools and strategies to adapt to new environments, great leaders continually evaluate and refine their approach. A new leader transition plan is the most effective tool to work through the key phases of equipping yourself, empowering your team, and delivering meaningful impact.

By organizing your efforts into these phases, you ensure that you're not just reacting to challenges but proactively moving toward success. As you complete each phase, re-equip yourself, empower others, and seek new opportunities to make an impact. The cycle never ends, and with each repetition, you sharpen your leadership tools and expand your capacity to lead with excellence.

Crisis Antidote Plans: "Plans are Worthless, but Planning is Everything"

During a speech in November 1957, President Dwight D. Eisenhower stated,

> Plans are worthless, but planning is everything. There is a very great distinction because when you are planning for an emergency you must start with this one thing: the very

definition of 'emergency' is that it is unexpected, therefore it is not going to happen the way you are planning.[32]

He emphasized that crises are often unforeseen, meaning they won't unfold as planned. *Every leader will face "rattlesnake" crises that seem to jump up and bite you out of nowhere.* The key is to be equipped with the antidote: a prepared response plan.

Leaders are the first ones people look to for answers in times of hardship and crisis, but they are also the first ones to be blamed.

Leaders often find themselves in situations where they don't have all the answers, such as managing a business during a pandemic or leading through personal crises. Regardless of the situation, leaders are expected to respond swiftly and effectively.

I've dealt with everything from fights to social media issues and sadly, even student suicides. The first time I faced each of these situations, I was overwhelmed, crying out to God for wisdom and strength. But over time, I learned how to better lead through these crisis moments (some better than others).

To better prepare yourself for the unknown, pack the following holistic remedy you and your team may need when responding to a crisis.

(Note: This information is not intended as a specific response procedure. You should be aware of and train your teams on your organization's multi-hazard emergency response procedures. If your organization doesn't have any, then advocate to have some put in place or visit your government's emergency management institutes for support.)

Generic Crisis Antidote for Leaders

1. Stay calm and check the scene for safety.
   When a situation arises, it's your job to maintain physical, emotional, and informational safety for everyone involved.

Never react hastily; instead, assess the scene and determine if there's a breach of safety or misinformation.
2. Neutralize the immediate threat.
Like administering an antidote, your response must focus on stabilizing the situation to prevent further damage. Establish calmness, structure, and clear communication. Address the issue decisively to prevent further harm. Inaction is not an option in moments of crisis.
3. Call for reinforcement and sustain your response.
No leader can handle every crisis alone. Reach out to mentors, organizational resources (like HR or communications), or external support systems. Stay present with your team to offer guidance, reassurance, and consistent engagement.
4. Recenter and recover.
Once the immediate threat has been neutralized, take time to recenter yourself. Processing your own emotions will help you sustain effective leadership for the long term.

Just as an antidote neutralizes venom, a proactive crisis plan allows leaders to mitigate the effects of unexpected challenges. Remember, every crisis faced and conquered makes you stronger, like a scar that tells the story of a lesson learned. As I often say, if someone claims to lead but doesn't walk with a limp, be cautious. The best leaders are those who've faced hardship, learned from it, and emerged better prepared for the challenges ahead.

Every tough situation teaches you something. Over time your anxiety will shrink, and your skills will grow. Take comfort in knowing that each challenge will pass—only to be replaced by another one. And that's okay. You will learn how to tackle each situation as it comes because that's what leaders do.

Leaders grow through hardships by learning from each situation and proactively mitigating future issues.

Never react like the sky is falling. Stay focused on what is mission critical and remember: What seems like a mountain today may just be a molehill tomorrow.

The hands of leadership represent action—the work that transforms plans into tangible outcomes and vision into reality. Execution is the bridge between strategy and results, requiring both precision and adaptability. Just as skilled hands wield tools to build, repair, and create, a leader's execution equips them to work through challenges, seize opportunities, and propel their team forward.

Every instrument in the execution multi-tool—whether it's a detailed plan, a proactive crisis response, or the systems and processes and service you refine along the way—serves to empower your leadership hands. They help you grip the challenges with confidence, shape the environment with purpose, and leave a legacy of meaningful progress.

By mastering execution, you demonstrate that leadership is not just about thinking and planning but about doing. Your hands hold the hatchet for cutting through complexity, the fire starter to spark inspiration and innovation, and the means to craft a path forward for your team. With execution as your ally, you'll not only achieve results but also build momentum, trust, and resilience along the way.

Take hold of your tools and put them to use—because great leadership is built through the hands that dare to act.

EXECUTION

Apply What You've Learned

- ☐ **Workbook**: Go through this chapter's section in the Leadership on the Rocks workbook.
- ☐ **Urgent/Important Matrix**: Look at your to-do list and categorize each task in the appropriate box on the Urgent/Important Matrix and take action accordingly.
- ☐ **Four principles of a plan**: Brain-dump (list) any problems, conflicts, or constraints you're experiencing. Focusing on one at a time, think through how you can implement these four principles:
  - ☐ Assess the situation first.
  - ☐ Establish structure to reduce chaos.
  - ☐ Provide clear communication.
  - ☐ Synthesize, summarize, and sustain your plan.
- ☐ **One-page plan**: Choose one problem to address and work towards a solution and rollout plan by using the one-page plan template found in the workbook.
- ☐ **New leader transition plan**: Prior to joining a new team, proactively plan how you will transition into that role.
- ☐ **First aid plan**: Prepare for the unexpected by proactively creating emergency or contingency plans.

CHAPTER 10

Systems and Processes

The Hatchet

LIKE ALL OTHER industries during the pandemic, the education world became a chaotic scene with everyone panicking about how to move forward in providing services for students despite the double-edged sword of government restrictions and government mandates. The swinging pendulum of dos and don'ts created massive complexities for educational systems everywhere.

During this tumultuous time, I considered it my number one job to help our school focus on the most mission-critical elements of what we did as an organization by working to simplify the complexities. I sat in meeting after meeting taking in massive amounts of information about all of the restrictions and mandates, but I couldn't in good conscience send our teachers into the dense forest of PowerPoints, memos, and never-ending requirements without first hacking away some of the superfluous details.

Before I sent anything to teachers, I had to use my execution tools to not only sharpen the focus on what was mission-critical information but to cut through the complexities and create a clear and viable path to allow us to continue providing quality education. It was the pandemic that taught me how to effectively use the hatchet of systems and processes to eliminate obstacles and streamline the work.

In the wilderness, a hatchet is an essential tool for survival. It hacks down dense underbrush, splits wood for a fire, and carves paths where none existed before. Small but mighty, the hatchet transforms obstacles into opportunities, turning what might seem impassable into something manageable. Without it, navigating the wilderness becomes a much more daunting task, and progress slows to a crawl.

Systems and processes are the hatchet in the hands of leadership execution. They are the tools that help you cut through the chaos of daily demands, clearing a path for productivity and progress. Just as a hatchet allows a survivalist to break down branches into usable materials, systems and processes break down overwhelming challenges into actionable steps.

With well-designed systems and streamlined processes, leaders can create clarity amidst complexity, reduce inefficiency, and ensure consistent progress. Without them, a leader's efforts become scattered, and their vision remains out of reach, obscured by obstacles that could have been cleared with the right tools. Systems and processes are not just about organization; they're about cutting away what's unnecessary so you can focus on what truly matters.

SYSTEMS AND PROCESSES

The Enemy of Progress

In the wilderness, leaving the underbrush untouched invites chaos—wild, untamed, and impossible to navigate. Without the hatchet to clear a path, you're left trapped by the status quo of nature. Similarly, in leadership, the real enemy of progress is not some external, mythical force; it's our own willingness to accept things as they stand.

When leaders fail to address inefficiencies, disorganization, or dysfunction, they allow chaos to fester like an overgrown forest. The clues that a team or organization has succumbed to the status quo are unmistakable: Chaos reigns, complaints echo, and fingers point in every direction. People observe the disorder but do nothing to change it, using confirmed biases or victim narratives to reinforce their inaction.

Instead of taking up the metaphorical hatchet to carve a new path, too many leaders settle for complaining about the thorns in their way. They may express a desire for positive change, but their actions—or lack thereof—tell a different story. They cast themselves as victims of circumstance, quick to explain intentions while naming villains who thwarted their plans.

But chaos left to thrive doesn't just slow progress; it destroys it. Like an untended wildfire, it breeds anxiety, stress, and conflict. Relationships break down, team morale plummets, productivity suffers, and results wither. Leaders who accept the status quo risk letting the chaos consume everything in its path.

Don't Play the Victim—Wield the Hatchet

Managers may accept the status quo, but leaders refuse to remain tangled in the brush. Instead, they take up the hatchet of leadership—systems and processes—to clear the way. They recognize that they hold the power to create progress and choose to step into the role of the hero. Heroes don't bemoan the challenges before them; they rise to meet them with grit, determination, and action.

Heroes and leaders alike accept the challenges before them, craft a plan, and use their tools—systems and processes—to cut through the chaos and restore peace. They refuse to let obstacles dictate their path; instead, they carve one of their own.

Don't settle for the chaos of the status quo. Take up the hatchet of systems and processes, and be the hero who cuts through obstacles, clears the path, and leads the way to a brighter, more efficient future.

The Hatchet of Leadership: Systems and Processes

Like a survivalist clearing dense brush to reach their destination, leaders use systems and processes to break down overwhelming challenges into manageable tasks. These tools create clarity, reduce friction, and ensure consistent progress. They allow leaders to address chaos head-on and transform it into opportunities for growth and success.

The Leadership on the Rocks Framework defines systems and processes this way: Systems are the *how* we work (most essential elements) and processes are the *what* we do for the work.

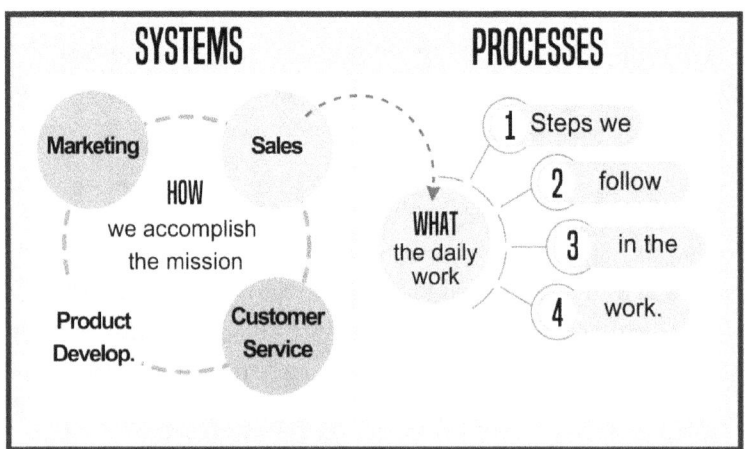

SYSTEMS AND PROCESSES

Together, systems and processes form the hatchet leaders use to cut through complexity, inefficiency, chaos, and stagnation, transforming them into actionable steps forward.

To be effective (achieving results), leaders must focus on the most mission-critical tasks. Systems and processes provide the structure and clarity to showcase what is important and how it will be accomplished.

People thrive on structure—whether they are your children, coworkers, or employees. Without structure and clarity, disorder takes hold, leading to poor execution and worse results. Leaders must prevent chaos by proactively creating systems that bring clarity and prioritize the right work.

To execute effectively, connect all aspects of work to produce flow—smooth, uninterrupted progress. Don't let obstacles control the work; instead, anticipate and prevent them with well-planned systems and processes. A mission-critical, simple structure will deliver results and empower your team.

Key Takeaway:

Building effective and efficient systems and processes streamlines work.

Systems

Systems are the critical *how* pieces of an organization's mission. They form the blade of the hatchet, cutting through complexity and chaos to provide a clear path forward. Without strong systems, leaders have no stable framework to rely on.

Think of an action movie where the hero's mission is to rescue a hostage. The hero wields their own "hatchet"—the systems of intelligence, surveillance, communications (comms), and supplies. These critical tools, though not flashy, are what enable the hero to achieve their goal.

In your organization, you may not be saving hostages, but you are on a mission. What are the essential systems your team needs to achieve its objectives? Define those elements clearly and ensure they are interconnected.

Disconnected systems—whether due to incompatible technology, unclear communication, or a lack of collaboration—create confusion, duplicate work, and poor execution. A well-designed, cohesive system ensures smooth, uninterrupted progress, much like a sharp hatchet cutting cleanly through obstacles.

Systems are the blade of the hatchet, stabilizing your mission by cutting through complexity and chaos. Take the time to sharpen your systems so they're strong and precise, giving your team the tools they need to succeed.

Processes

If systems are the blade of the hatchet (the *how*), then processes are the precise strokes it takes to cut through the challenges (the *what*). Processes are the detailed steps required to turn your systems into action.

Think of processes as the grip on the hatchet's handle—the part that ensures you can swing with control and precision. Without a solid grip, even the sharpest blade is useless. Similarly, without well-defined processes, even the best systems will falter.

Processes should always be *standardized* (consistent across the team or organization) and *simple* (clear and easy to follow so they can be implemented effectively).

Avoid overcomplicating processes. Neither a hatchet with an unwieldy handle nor a process with fifty unnecessary steps will be effective. Aim for simplicity to ensure success.

Ultimately, the success of your processes determines the effectiveness of your systems—and the achievement of your mission.

You cannot approach a mission hoping for the best. Be intentional in planning for the best. By developing clear processes, your team will know exactly *what* they need to do every day to move the systems forward and accomplish the mission. With a strong grip on the hatchet's handle, your team will thrive under structure, make meaningful progress, and leave disorganization and conflict behind.

Building the Structure for Execution

Now that you understand systems and processes, let's explore how to create them within your team or organization. Without structure, chaos will reign—and with it comes conflict.

The hatchet metaphor is clear: Structure is the handle that allows you to wield the blade effectively. A strong, well-crafted handle ensures precision and control, helping you cut through disarray and create clarity. To build this structure, follow these five steps: listen, identify, define, train, and refine.

1. **Listen**

    A sharp leader listens before acting. Your team knows the challenges they face and often has valuable insights into potential solutions. Instead of assuming you have all the answers, gather feedback to uncover the real issues and opportunities. Ask these four questions:
    - What do you do? (roles and daily activities)
    - What is working well? (actions that contribute to the mission)
    - What is not working well? (time-wasting tasks, inefficiencies, or lack of support)
    - What would you remove, add, or change? (ways to improve efficiency and effectiveness)

    There are a few caveats:
    - If you lead a large team, consider gathering input through surveys or small group discussions. You can then follow up with your staff in a team meeting or town hall.

- An emotionally safe environment (like an anonymous survey) encourages honest feedback. Be prepared for a flood of negativity where *all* the problems could be voiced—this is evidence of pent-up frustration, not a reflection that "everything sucks."
- Feedback will range from insightful to self-serving (e.g., "That's not my job so give it to another department.") Not every idea will be actionable, but the goal is to uncover patterns, foster openness, and find the gems that can drive progress.

2. **Identify**

    Once you've gathered feedback, identify the essential, mission-critical elements. You'll likely uncover outdated practices, inefficient habits ("we've always done it this way"), and communication gaps. These pain points often reveal the missing links in your systems.

    Stay focused on what's most important to the organization as a whole—not just to individual departments. Ensure all the systems are interconnected, creating a smooth flow from one to the next. This step is vital for eliminating silos and aligning the work.

3. **Define**

    Efficient organizations have clear, standardized procedures of operations (SPOs). This clarity ensures everyone understands their role and how it fits into the bigger picture.

    Using the insights from the previous steps, define your systems and processes. Create a *process map*—a visual guide showing how work moves from start to finish.

    Figures one and two are examples of process maps. Keep your processes simple and sustainable. Overcomplicated, multistep instructions are the enemy of implementation. Aim for clarity and practicality.

SYSTEMS AND PROCESSES

A process map is also an excellent onboarding tool and helps stakeholders understand their journey within your organization's framework.

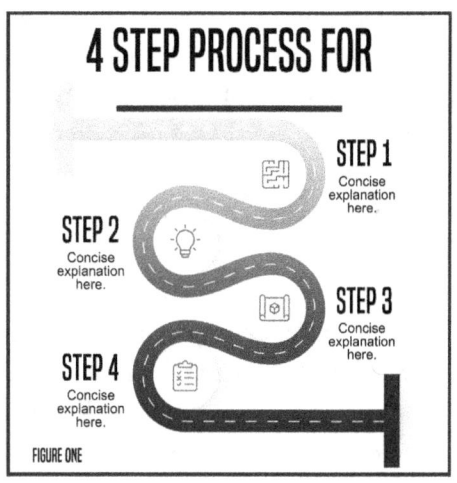

4. **Train**

   Your hatchet won't cut if no one knows how to use it. Once systems and processes are defined, ensure your team is trained to implement them effectively.

   Training isn't a one-and-done event. To best help team members thrive you must provide *time* for learning and practicing the processes and *support* for ongoing coaching and feedback.

   Leaders who equip their teams with the tools and knowledge they need to succeed reduce chaos and increase confidence.

5. **Refine**

   Even the best processes can be improved. After your team gets the hang of the structure, empower them to suggest refinements to make it more efficient. Ensure these changes are approved and standardized across the organization.

Starting Small: Tackling the Hot Spots

If your team feels like a hot mess, don't get overwhelmed. Start by identifying the "hot spots"—the pain points causing the most frustration. Make a prioritized list and begin with one area.

Taking that first step to establish clarity and structure—whether through sharpening systems, refining processes, or both—can transform your team. Being the leader who takes action is always better than standing still and complaining about the status quo.

The hatchet is in your hands. Use it wisely.

Streamlining the Work

Now that we've explored how to be effective (getting the work done), let's turn our attention to being efficient—maximizing results while minimizing wasted resources. Efficiency in leadership is like clearing a trail: The goal is to find the clearest path between points A and D, reducing obstacles and energy drains along the way.

Streamlining the work means focusing on the most essential and effective elements while eliminating unnecessary steps or distractions. As Greg McKeown suggests in *Effortless*, ask yourself, *What if this could be easy?*[33]

McKeown's question highlights a truth: We often overcomplicate things, but simplicity leads to success. What if the work could be easier to implement and more connected while still getting the desired results?

Common Roadblocks to Streamlining Work

Before we simplify, we need to recognize obstacles that disrupt flow and interconnectedness. These barriers are like loose rocks along the trail—they may seem small, but they can trip us up:

Too many steps within a process	Like pebbles in a shoe, they cause pain and slow progress.
Overly possessive of the work	Similar to a basketball player who refuses to pass the ball, this limits team success.
Lack of clarity on the goal	Imagine trying to assemble a thousand-piece puzzle without seeing the picture on the box.
Too many choices	Like the endless cereal aisle, it leads to paralysis and indecision.
Reluctance to make decisions	Bureaucratic stalling is like standing still on the trail and blaming others for your lack of progress.

Frequent shifts in direction	Rapid "pendulum swings" from one initiative to the next create stops and starts that derail momentum.

Without clarity and connection, employees end up working harder and longer but still leave feeling unaccomplished. This frustration stems from work that isn't streamlined or sustainable.

Breaking Free from the Chaos

In most organizations, new mandates, procedures, and processes are constantly added, but rarely is anything removed. These layers of complexity weigh down teams and create unnecessary stress. The solution? Shift your approach to streamline the work using these tactics:

Focus on the Vital Few

Start by shrinking the work of your team, just as you've done with your personal to-do list. Michael Hyatt, in *Free to Focus*, emphasizes the importance of how we spend our time and encourages us to say "no" more often. His framework—eliminate, automate, and delegate—offers a great roadmap to remove things from our schedules.[34]

As a leader, you have the authority to prioritize what's essential and say no to non-mission-critical tasks. Be intentional about designing processes that are both streamlined and sustainable.

Simplify with KISS

Remember the KISS principle: Keep it simple, stupid. Ask your team, "How can we KISS this process?" This question helps distinguish essential steps from fluff, ensuring the work is both efficient and impactful.

Build Collaborative Teams

Collaboration is the backbone of streamlined work. Teams that communicate and plan together at the start of a project save time, resources, and confusion later. Asking, "How can we collaborate better within our team and across departments?" can uncover redundancies and reduce busywork.

Leading the Way

As a leader, you have the power to clear the trail for your team, removing obstacles and ensuring the journey is smooth and connected. Streamlining the work isn't just about efficiency; it's about creating a sustainable path that allows your team to thrive. Remember, simplicity isn't just a luxury; it's a necessity for long-term success.

As a leader, your ultimate goal is to improve outcomes—whether that's boosting results, increasing profits, raising scores, or enhancing quality of life and service. However, leadership isn't about doing the day-to-day work yourself. Instead, it's about supporting your team in *how* they will do the work to achieve those outcomes.

When you establish systems and processes, you create a structure that reduces disorder and confusion. By streamlining those systems, you ensure that every effort focuses on the most essential and impactful elements, maximizing efficiency while conserving resources.

Remember, people thrive with clarity and structure. Providing your team with efficient systems not only enhances productivity but also fosters confidence and reduces frustration. Equip yourself with the hatchet of systems and processes to simplify, connect, and elevate the work, making it effective, efficient, and results-driven.

Leadership isn't about doing more—it's about doing *better*. With the right tools, you can lead your team to success, ensuring every effort aligns with your goals and vision.

Apply What You've Learned

- ☐ **Workbook**: Go through this chapter's section in the Leadership on the Rocks workbook.
- ☐ **Systems**: What systems are currently in place for the scope of your work? Are any missing? Do some need to be removed?
- ☐ **Processes**: What processes are currently in place for day-to-day work? Are any missing? Do some need to be removed?
- ☐ **Creating structure**: Establish structure to reduce the chaos and conflict around the work.
  - ☐ Listen: Gather information from your team on the current work being done and the challenges they are experiencing.
  - ☐ Identify: Work with your team to identify what mission-critical elements are present and which ones are missing in the current work.
  - ☐ Define: Develop standardized procedures of operations (SPOs) for quality assurance and efficacy.
  - ☐ Train: Provide training for implementation of the processes. Remember to add ample time for questions and coaching.
  - ☐ Refine: Allow your team members to have the autonomy to refine the processes they work with so that they can make them efficient.
- ☐ **Process maps:** Create a process map diagram that shows the most essential systems/processes of how the service/process gets from point A (conception) to point D (delivered to the stakeholder).

SYSTEMS AND PROCESSES

- **Streamline the work**: Create the best path between points A and D of the work. The best path will have the least amount of resistance but will also achieve the biggest return on the resources invested.
- Focus on the vital few: Talk with your team members about the work and ask what can be eliminated, automated, or delegated.
- Simplify with KISS (Keep it simple, stupid): Ask your team how the processes can be simplified.
- Build collaborative teams: Create a RACI chart for the next collaborative project.

CHAPTER 11

Service

The Match

WHEN I WAS growing up, my parents owned a pizza restaurant, and I was practically raised in it. From a young age, I was serving guests and clearing tables, learning firsthand the importance of customer service. One of the most valuable lessons I carried with me into my professional life was that customer service matters. It has the power to create an experience that not only fulfills everyone involved but also fosters loyalty and meaningful engagement.

As I transitioned from running a high school to launching my own leadership coaching business, I found that while systems and processes are crucial, they are most effective when paired with the warmth of great customer service. Whether it's a frontline employee or a high-level executive, focusing on creating a positive experience in every interaction helps ignite a flame—one that spreads joy, trust, openness, and loyalty across an organization and community.

In the wilderness, a campfire is more than just a tool for survival; it's the heart of the experience. It provides light in the darkness, warmth against the cold, and a gathering place for reflection and connection. Without it, the night would be colder and more isolating, with no sense of comfort or camaraderie to bring people together.

Service acts as the match to light that campfire. In leadership, service is the spark that ignites connection, belonging, and unity. Like a campfire, service requires intentional effort to keep it burning brightly. A fire needs kindling, logs, and oxygen just as service needs action, consistency, and care. Without service, the flame of connection begins to fade, leaving teams fragmented, leaders disconnected, and stakeholders complaining.

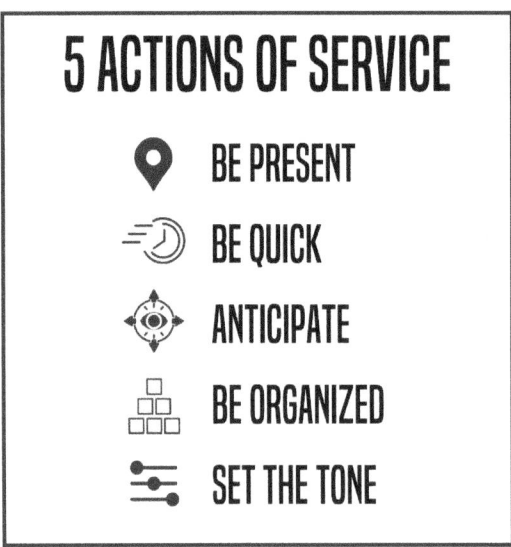

SERVICE

This is why service is such an essential tool in the Leadership on the Rocks survival kit. As a leader, service is the outward-facing cultural center of your leadership. It fosters trust, collaboration, and loyalty—the foundational elements that sustain long-term success. Just as a campfire draws people close, service draws your team together, inspiring them to unite around a common purpose and move forward with renewed strength. Without it, a leader is like a camper in the cold—adrift in isolation, unable to light the way for others.

The Leadership on the Rocks Framework defines service as simply taking action, helping, or doing work for the benefit of others.

Key Takeaway:

Quality service creates a better environment where the why, how, and what of work can be fully realized.

I know many leaders understand that servant leadership is important—it's often as unquestioned as answers like "Jesus" or "pray" in faith-related questions. But I also want to make a clear distinction between what service is and isn't. When I was younger in leadership, I thought being a servant leader meant always giving in to others' will and being passive. But I quickly learned how wrong I was on both counts. Serving is about focusing on others, but it does not mean always bending to the will of others.

In reality, service leadership is active, intentional, and strong-willed. As Dan Cathy, the chairman of Chick-Fil-A, says, "Selfless, servant leadership is about action, and the bottom line is that what we say and what we believe will only be as effective as what we are also willing to do."[35] Service is about action, and it distinguishes great leaders from the good and the great companies from the rest.

Whether I'm talking about fast-food chicken, buying paint, visiting a doctor's office, or working in a leadership role, it's clear that organizations and leaders who focus on service are the ones that attract loyalty and commitment. People flock to them, willing to spend their money, time, and talents. The difference is in the service provided—the warmth that fuels relationships and builds lasting connections.

To provide quality service, no matter your industry or leadership role, there are five essential actions we need to take: be present, be quick, anticipate, be organized, and set the tone. These actions are not just about serving; they are about creating a space where the match of service can light the fire of connection, trust, and success.

1. Be Present

The first action to provide quality service is to be present—engaged and visible. It's not a complicated concept, yet it's one that can easily be overlooked. To be present means to be fully engaged with the people around you, noticing and interacting with them.

On the other hand, being present doesn't mean just occupying space. For example, sitting in a meeting, checking emails on your phone or laptop—this is not being present. That's just taking up space while your attention is elsewhere.

Whether in meetings or on the ground with your team, your presence matters. Your team, customers, and stakeholders want to engage with you. They need your leadership, your inspiration, and your feedback.

You may be yelling at the book, "But Bethany, you don't know how many emails and meetings I have!"

I hear you! Emails and meetings are a heavy load for today's leaders. *But here's the truth: For those of you overwhelmed by emails and meetings, it's not a time problem; it's a priority problem.* Your people are more important than your email, and honestly, they're more important than those meetings that drain your energy without moving the needle. Don't let the noise of unimportant tasks drown out the essentials.

Hear my heart on this because what I'm about to tell you is life-changing: *No one owns you. Every action you take is a choice.* You own your time and calendar, so choose to schedule your priorities. Block time on your calendar for being present with your people, and don't let anyone schedule over this time. At bare minimum, set an alarm on your phone to remind you to get up and walk the floor to go see your team, employees, customers, or stakeholders.

Take action: Make time to be present and engage with those you serve.

2. Be Quick

Providing quality service also means being quick. But don't worry, I'm not talking about your sprinting ability.

Service action number two is about being quick to respond to situations and needs, whether they're good or bad.

You'd be surprised how easily this can happen if you've mastered action number one. When you are present and fully engaged, you'll start noticing things you never saw before. You'll develop a "sixth sense" for what's happening around you that will help you respond more quickly.

Let me share an example from my education days. School administrators often spend their days and nights on duty, supervising students and the public at school events. Great administrators who are engaged with their environment can read the attitudes, feelings, and behaviors of hundreds of students (or parents) around them. This allows them to respond promptly, preventing situations from escalating. I can't tell you how many "almost fights" were avoided because a good administrator was present and quick to act.

In the business world, when leaders are present and engaged, they rarely face unexpected bombshells. Because they're engaged, they have a better sense of when things are going wrong, and they can prepare and respond quickly.

But what about a positive scenario? Let's say your customers are loving your product, so much so that they are telling their friends. If you're present and engaged, you can sense the growing demand and act quickly to meet it. This means ensuring production can handle the increased orders and that customer service reps are ready to serve more clients.

Leaders who provide great service are quick to respond to the needs of their employees and customers. And that builds loyalty.

3. Anticipate

We've covered being present and responding quickly, but actions three, four, and five are the crème de la crème of service. When you reach a point in your leadership and relationships where you can "see around the corner" and proactively address what lies ahead, you're operating at the highest level of service for your employees, customers, and stakeholders.

Service action number three is to anticipate the needs of others.

When it comes to leadership, you're dealing with two key things: leading people and managing tasks.

Action number three focuses on the people-side of leadership. As a leader, you need to think ahead about what your team, customers, and stakeholders might need before they ask for it.

While you can't anticipate everything, you can take a moment to pause and reflect. Put yourself in the shoes of your employees, customers, and stakeholders, and think about what they might need, what challenges they might face, or what questions they may have.

This is where emotional intelligence sets great leaders apart. Think of it like this: When you go to a restaurant, the best waiters are the ones who refill your drink before it's empty or bring more bread before you finish the last piece.

In leadership, anticipate the needs or problems your customers might face and plan how you can solve them before they ask. Be proactive with the information your stakeholders want and answer their questions before they even ask them.

The pandemic tested leaders like never before. The leaders who survived and thrived were those who were present and engaged, quick to respond, and able to anticipate the needs of their stakeholders.

When you activate your empathy and emotional intelligence, you can serve others proactively. Think of this action as being ready to add fuel to the fire before it starts to die down—keeping it burning brightly before anyone notices a flicker.

4. Be Organized

Action number four for providing great service is to create organized systems and processes for efficiency.

In leadership, it's essential to balance both the people side and the task side of things. Service action three (anticipate) focuses on the people side, while action four is about ensuring the task side runs smoothly.

Organizing systems and processes is a key part of providing effective and efficient service. But here's the twist—these systems don't just help you; they also help your customers and stakeholders by making their experience more seamless.

Think about Amazon, a company renowned for its efficient systems and logistics. They have organized processes that allow them to deliver fast and reliable service to millions of customers worldwide. By using cutting-edge technology and a well-structured work environment, they ensure streamlined operations that lead to exceptional customer experiences.

Let me reveal two secrets that produce superior service from all people:

1. People thrive in structured environments.
2. People will rise to the level of the expectations placed on them.

Where there is no structure or clear expectation, things will always fall apart, rendering terrible service.

When employees understand the system and have the tools to do their job efficiently, they can serve others well. Similarly, when your organization has structured systems in place, you'll be able to better meet customer expectations.

The key here is that systems and processes keep your "fire" of service burning brightly. When your operations run smoothly, everyone's experience improves, and your leadership becomes more effective.

5. Set the Tone

The final action to create great service is to set the tone with a positive and loving attitude.

As Pastor Charles Swindoll said, "Life is 10 percent what happens to you and 90 percent how you react."[36] You can't always control your circumstances, but you can control your attitude. This is crucial when it comes to leading and serving others.

People are always buying into you and your energy.

Just like a campfire, the atmosphere you create can change the environment around you. Your attitude—whether positive or negative—affects the energy of the room and the people in it. Leaders who exude positivity help others perform better, while negative attitudes can drag everyone down.

That's why service action number five—having a positive and loving attitude—is essential. Positivity inspires hope, and love builds bridges in difficult times. Your attitude has the power to ignite passion and enthusiasm in those around you.

In a world where problems seem to pop up out of nowhere, you can't always control your circumstances, but you can control how you respond. By leading with a positive attitude, you can help your team face challenges with optimism and purpose.

In summary, the five actions of service—being present, being quick to respond, anticipating needs, staying organized, and setting the tone—are the matches for the leader's hands to create a positive experience for those you serve. When you integrate these actions into your leadership, you not only strengthen your relationships but also cultivate an environment where people thrive. Now, let's turn our attention to another critical aspect of leadership: protecting the workday.

Protect the Workday

There are little thieves at work that are stealing our time and energy, and, like a fire deprived of fuel, these distractions rob our team's focus and productivity. These thieves aren't only the outward-facing tasks that steal from customers and stakeholders, but the internal issues that drain the resources of our most valuable asset: the people.

Who are these thieves? The biggest culprits that often go unchecked are emails and meetings.

As a leader, it's your responsibility and authority to protect the workday and guard your team from these distractions. Like the matches in a leader's hands, your proactive actions can kindle a positive, productive fire of collaboration and focus where your team can truly thrive.

Emails

Let's talk about the overuse of email, one of the greatest thieves at work, stealing not only our time but also our focus and energy. Our inboxes are like the nagging gnats of the office, constantly buzzing around and distracting us from our work. The sheer quantity of unnecessary emails—especially the dreaded "CC" culture—snuffs out the fire of productivity, draining your team's time and energy.

Essentially, this "CC" email culture is saying that if I copy everyone on every email, I'll never have to take responsibility for problems because I supposedly "communicated" about them. This is an absolute fallacy.

In our heads, we justify it by saying, "It's not my fault that 'Bethany' didn't know. I copied her on that one email, six months ago. She should have known this widget was a problem."

The quantity of email is breaking down communication within your organization. When people are overwhelmed by constant emails, they are robbed of the time they could have spent focusing on tasks that actually move the organization forward.

Better communication and service happen through a two-minute conversation, not a twenty-email thread.

As a leader, it's your responsibility to protect your team's workday by redefining your email culture and setting clear expectations. Implement email etiquette such as limiting most emails to six lines or less, restricting the use of "reply all," and encouraging direct conversations over back-and-forth email exchanges. Establish boundaries for when emails should and should not be checked—such as after hours or on weekends. By doing this, you not only protect your team's time but also eliminate the frustration that comes with a bloated inbox, ensuring that you keep the fire of productivity burning.

Meetings

"This meeting was a waste of my time and energy," said every employee ever about most meetings. How much time do you spend in meetings within a given day or week? The truth is most of our workplace meetings suck. They suck away our time. They suck our energy. They suck our morale, productivity, and even our results and profits. Bad meetings are like a fire that's been doused, snuffing out progress and leaving behind wasted time and frustration.

Long, drawn-out meetings with no purpose waste time, money, and resources. Time is money! If organizations put an hourly cost on a meeting invite based on the hourly wage of its participants, everyone would be shocked at how much "money" is spent per meeting. For example, a one-hour meeting between five people making fifty dollars per hour costs the organization $250. Yet, the work that those employees could have done instead of attending the meeting could have saved the company thousands.

As a leader, it's your job to eliminate what doesn't generate a return on your team's time. The first step is having fewer, but more effective and efficient, meetings. Hosting an effective meeting isn't rocket science. It just requires intentionality and a focus on what's essential—and this is where agendas come in.

While agendas help provide clarity and flow, not all agendas are created equal. You must know how to use them effectively, and here are four key steps for planning and hosting a more productive meeting:

1. Know *why* the meeting is necessary and *who* needs to attend. If the meeting's purpose doesn't directly tie into your team's mission or goals, it could be handled with an email or collaborative document instead. Also, if the key participants aren't available, consider canceling the meeting.
2. Decide the *where* and *what* of the meeting. Will it be in person or virtual? What topics are mission critical and need to be placed on the agenda?
3. Determine *how* the meeting will be run. Are you simply informing the team about an issue? Or do you need to discuss something in depth or make a decision?
4. Set norms and prepare pre-reads. Send out the agenda ahead of time so everyone can come prepared to inform, discuss, or decide. Clear expectations on how to engage make for a more productive meeting.

In addition to these steps, *set time limits*. Remember, like water, communication can sustain, but it can also drown. If you don't place limits on time, topics can spill out of control and waste valuable time.

Finally, *end the meeting well by providing a recap* (or sending an email recap). Briefly summarize what was discussed, the decisions made, action items delegated, and timelines created.

By following these strategies, you can reduce unnecessary meetings and make the ones that remain more efficient, protecting your team's time and energy while keeping the fire of productivity alive.

To wrap it up, protecting your team's time is an essential part of serving them well. By removing unnecessary distractions like emails and poorly planned meetings, you create space for your team to focus on what truly matters. This is how you protect the workday—just like tending to a fire, you must carefully manage the fuel to keep the flames burning bright.

No matter the industry or our title, our goal should always be to serve our employees, customers, and stakeholders well. Quality service is foundational to a thriving leadership environment where the *why*, *how*, and *what* of the work are clearly understood and implemented.

Great service doesn't mean giving in to every unreasonable demand. Instead, it's about focusing on the most essential "big rocks" that align with your values and vision. As leaders, we are here to serve those in our care; this requires an others-focused mindset. Just as a match sparks the fire that fuels progress, service is the match that ignites the flames of trust and engagement.

By taking intentional action to serve, whether it's through listening, anticipating needs, or protecting our team's time, we keep the fire of

SERVICE

productivity burning bright. As we continue to pack our Leadership on the Rocks survival kit, remember that service is not just an action but a mindset that sets the tone for everything that follows.

Apply What You've Learned

- ☐ **Workbook**: Go through this chapter's section in the Leadership on the Rocks workbook.
- ☐ **Be present**: Schedule times to be visible and engage with all of your stakeholders.
- ☐ **Be quick**: Is there a situation you've noticed that you need to respond to? Make a plan now and take action to respond.
- ☐ **Anticipate**: What are your customers, partners, and employees going through (or about to go through)? How can you anticipate their needs, questions, problems, etc.?
- ☐ **Be organized**: Create a customer journey map to think through the work from their perspective. Is there anything you need to adjust within the work to provide a better customer experience?
- ☐ **Set the tone**: Reflect on your current attitude and energy? Are you giving off positive or negative energy?
- ☐ **Protect the workday**: Think through the chaotic parts of the day. What is stealing the employee's time? How can you eliminate those distractions?
  - ☐ Emails: Create email etiquette guidelines for your team.
  - ☐ Meetings: Look at the previous weeks and months on your calendar. What meetings were a waste of time? Eliminate those meetings in the future.
  - ☐ Agendas: Create an agenda that will cultivate an efficient and effective meeting.

PART 5

The Guts of Leadership

Building, Defending, and Sustaining Prosperity

CHAPTER 12

Accountability

The Shelter

I AM PRETTY CONSISTENT with proactive communication. When I was the gradebook administrator, I would send out reminders weeks ahead of time, making sure staff had everything they needed. Yet despite my best efforts, at the end of every grading period, a handful of educators still missed deadlines or didn't even have grades entered into the system. I remember staring at the grading report and wondering how an employee could not perform their job. It was in that moment I realized the importance of holding others accountable for their responsibilities.

Fast forward to a few years later. I was facilitating a meeting when one frustrated employee stood up and yelled an inappropriate name at a coworker. In an instant, the coworker responded in kind. I ended the meeting immediately, shocked and wondering how professionals could behave like that. That moment taught me the necessity of stepping into difficult conversations when behaviors fall short of ethical or professional expectations.

Over time, my shock-face in circumstances like these faded, and I grew stronger in handling tough conversations. But I also learned that proactive accountability measures were just as essential as reactive ones. Accountability isn't just about addressing mistakes after they happen; it's about creating a framework to protect the team from conflicts, misunderstandings, and misaligned behaviors before they occur.

Leadership often feels like camping in unpredictable terrain. The winds of conflict, rainstorms of doubt, and blazing heat of pressure can challenge even the most resilient teams. That's why we need to protect the guts of leadership with the shelter of accountability. By packing our Leadership on the Rocks survival kit with this crucial structure, we can create a safe yet challenging environment where growth can thrive.

The tent, historically, has served as a symbol of both stability and shelter, refuge and resolution. In leadership, the tent represents this dual role: a place of clarity and strategy but also a space where tough decisions are made and alignment is maintained.

Just as a tent requires strong stakes and poles to stand, accountability demands clarity, commitment, and the courage to engage in difficult conversations. Without these, even the best-intentioned leaders risk exposing their teams to conflict, confusion, and inefficiency.

Stepping Into the Shelter: How Accountability Grounds Leadership

Leadership is hard. Leading in a crisis is hard. Working through conflict is hard. Addressing poor performance is hard. Taking ownership

ACCOUNTABILITY

of something that didn't go well is hard. Stepping into the proverbial "shelter" of tough situations—whether it's a crisis, conflict, or poor performance—is what leadership is truly all about.

Just like a tent or cave offers shelter from unpredictable conditions, accountability provides the structure and framework we need to lead with clarity, responsibility, and integrity. Leaders take responsibility for everyone and everything within their care, and stepping into the tent of accountability means confronting issues head-on, even when it's uncomfortable.

In this chapter, we'll explore how to tackle the situations that might tempt us to ignore or avoid them. Accountability is a shelter that covers not just the behavior and performance of those we lead but also our own.

Just like a tent can weather a storm, strong accountability helps us weather the challenges that arise in leadership and in turn, protects the stability and culture of our teams and organizations. By defending a culture of accountability, we are not only protecting the internal environment but also positioning our organization for positive growth that can extend into the wider community.

Consider the task of getting children to clean their rooms. While there may be occasional joy in the act, it's often teeming with resistance. Many times I'd ask my children to clean their rooms, and when I'd inspect their work, I'd find the usual pattern. Things looked neat on the surface, but beneath the bed, in the closets, or in the drawers, clutter was still lurking. There were two reasons for this: Either they had grown used to the mess and didn't notice it anymore, or they simply didn't want to deal with it and tried to "sweep it under the rug."

As leaders, it's easy to fall into the trap of ignoring the mess or sweeping it under the rug, hoping it will resolve itself. But just as in our homes, we cannot afford to ignore the disarray in our organizations. Leadership requires us to step into the tent of accountability, face the mess head-on, and address it proactively.

Whether it's dealing with poor performance, ethical violations, or unresolved conflict, we must resist the temptation to "hide" these issues and instead take responsibility for them. We are called to be torchbearers of accountability, leading by example and taking ownership of both our actions and the actions of those in our care.

Much like Superman is vulnerable to kryptonite, leaders can be noble and powerful until they face conflict or accountability—then they can lose their effectiveness. When leaders avoid difficult conversations or ignore performance issues, they lose credibility and the trust of their teams. Accountability is the strength that holds the tent upright, keeping us stable and grounded even during the toughest storms.

Key Takeaway:

Leaders speak up about things that matter.

When you avoid accountability, you are undermining your leadership and allowing negative behaviors or poor performance to take root. Teams are always watching. They know when leaders turn a blind eye, sending the message that certain behaviors or performance levels are acceptable. This makes the work experience—as my husband's friend James Findley often says—"fraught with peril."

Ignoring situations only deteriorates team culture and leadership effectiveness. Just like inaction is a form of action, ignoring accountability is a decision that will have consequences.

Inaction Is an Action

On March 7, 1965, a day after the horrific Bloody Sunday events in Selma, Alabama, Dr. Martin Luther King Jr. delivered a speech about the importance of standing up for what is right and just, no matter the consequence of doing so. Dr. King said, "A man dies when he refuses to stand up for that which is right."[37]

Today this speech by Dr. King is often known by its paraphrased quote: "Our lives begin to end the day we become silent about things that matter."

This summary expresses a truth we cannot deny: Leaders cannot be silent or inactive about important things.

Remember, leadership isn't tied to a title but a level of influence.

Lyndon Pryor, president and CEO of the Louisville Urban League, shared on my *Leadership on the Rocks* podcast that everyone sits at a table (or multiple tables) in which they have power, position, and the opportunity to shift the conversation. Whether at work, at home, or within social circles, everyone sits at a table and has an opportunity to lead by speaking up about things that matter.[38]

People watch and emulate leaders of influence, so it is important that leaders don't stay silent and that they don't play the victim, attributing silence to an assertion that there was nothing they could do.

Leaders should never fear speaking up and taking action for what is right. Unfortunately, beyond clear questions of right and wrong, fear often keeps leaders silent. I've witnessed leaders hesitate to challenge outdated, ineffective, or "sacred" programs simply because they feared rejection or backlash from higher-ups. This kind of hesitation stifles progress and undermines the purpose of leadership.

In her book *Braving the Wilderness*, Brené Brown shares an insightful call to action in how we handle adversity; she calls us to have a "Strong back. Soft front. Wild heart."[39] This phrase has become one of my favorite mantras for leadership.

Leaders, we are called to have a strong back. That is the number one thing you need to not be crushed by the weight of responsibility, problems, conflicts, and constraints that come with the position of leadership. Yes, people are looking to you to make the first move—you are the leader—you must go first. Going first requires a strong backbone. But we're also called to be tender in how we engage with people.

Leadership demands resilience, courage, and empathy in equal measure.

Leaders must be steadfast in shouldering responsibility and taking action, even when it's uncomfortable, because the first action of accountability always falls to the leader. For example, when employee performance falters, the leader must always ask if it is due to a lack of clarity, structure, training, or feedback. If the answer is yes, then the accountability lies with the leader, and action must take place in those areas.

However, if the issue stems from a lack of skill, motivation, or insubordination on behalf of the employee, then the accountability lies with him or her. Employees may choose not to perform or be unable to perform; as a leader, you don't own the cause of their poor performance, but you will definitely own the effects of it.

In the end, no matter the cause of the issue that needs to be addressed, the leader must take action. They must approach others with respect and compassion, recognizing that how we treat people during difficult conversations leaves a lasting impact. And above all, leaders must summon the bravery to stand firm, even when their decisions are not popular or widely understood.

Accountability is about making the tough calls that drive growth and progress. It requires having ownership of mistakes, responsibility for what must be done, flexibility in implementing best practices, and creativity in exploring new possibilities. Good leaders embrace accountability as part of their stewardship; they face challenges head-on and lead with both conviction and integrity.

When faced with tough decisions, gather input, evaluate the situation honestly, and take ownership of the path forward. Leadership means holding yourself and others accountable, even when those above you don't.

Conflict Conversations

The majority of this book teaches proactive actions you must take to set yourself and your team up for success in the area of accountability. But now we need to face reality: people aren't perfect.

As a leader, your greatest asset is your people, but they can also be your biggest headache when it comes to conflict and accountability conversations. Wherever there are people, there will be conflict and unmet expectations.

No one gets it right 100 percent of the time, including you and me. Unfortunately, human nature—pride and selfishness—doesn't naturally prompt us to see our own faults or own our mistakes.

Enter conflict.

It's our responsibility as leaders to step into tough conversations to resolve conflict, hold people accountable, and model effective problem-solving dialogue. The problem? Many leaders lack the skills needed to model and navigate these conversations effectively. Too often accountability discussions turn into counterproductive tit-for-tat exchanges.

Stepping into conflict and accountability conversations is hard—rock hard. That's where the AC/DC method comes in. (See what I did there?)

The AC/DC method equips leaders to resolve conflict, find resolution and reconciliation, and establish a clear path forward.

Here's the beauty of this method: Most of the work for resolving conflict or holding someone accountable happens *in your head* before you ever speak to the employee!

Protect Yourself and Others

Before diving into the AC/DC method, a critical note: If you're dealing with a disgruntled or insubordinate employee, or if the issue involves a significant incident, protect yourself and everyone involved by bringing in a third-party witness. The witness should be someone in a position of authority but not the direct supervisor of those involved.

The AC/DC Method

1. Accept

The first step is accepting that you *must* have the difficult conversation. Use mental strategies—like mantras, prayer, or talking to mentors—to help you embrace this reality.

Hard conversations can be stressful and anxiety-inducing for everyone. Do the mental work to accept that mediating conflict and holding people accountable is an essential part of leadership.

2. Check

Next, check your ego. Ego can sabotage conflict mediation.

Human nature drives us to be selfish and prideful, crafting mental stories where we're the hero or victim and others are the villains. Great leaders must rise above these tendencies.

Conflict and accountability conversations are emotionally charged—like dodgeball, with emotions flying everywhere. Add dominance or disrespect to the mix, and you've got a disaster. Use your leadership mindset to stay calm and respond thoughtfully instead of reacting emotionally.

In these conversations, the right (and legal) thing to do is give each party an opportunity to share their perspective. Prepare to listen, ask clarifying questions, and listen again before responding.

3. Decide

Identify the root cause of the conflict before entering the conversation.

ACCOUNTABILITY

Whether you're directly involved or mediating for others, you need to decide what part of the conflict you will address and what outcome you hope to achieve.

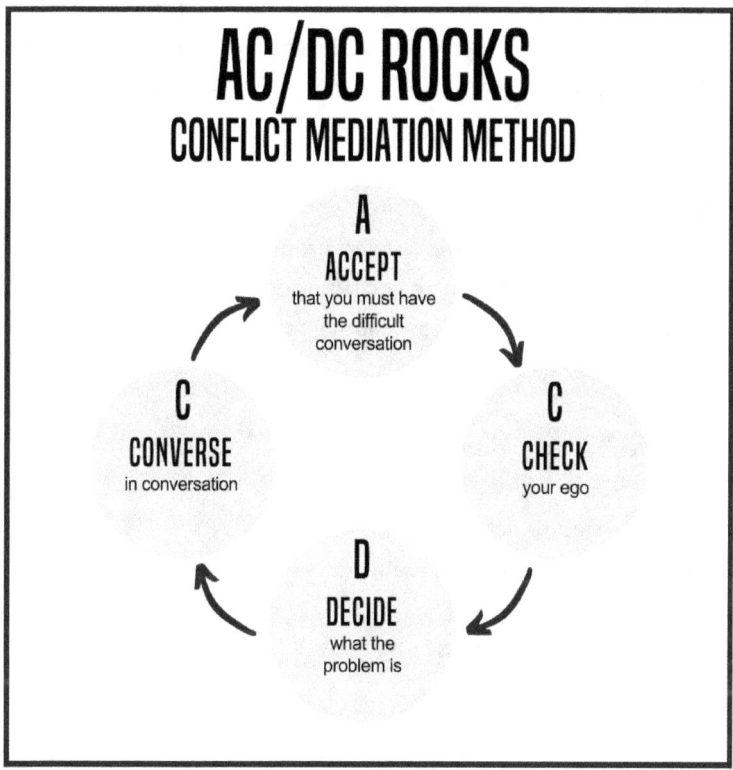

Patterson, Grenny, and their co-authors in *Crucial Accountability* emphasize the importance of addressing the right issue.[40] Don't approach the conversation with a "charcuterie board" of grievances. Focus on one specific issue.

Think of the problem as a ball—you can throw one ball and expect someone to catch it, but throwing multiple balls at once guarantees a miss.

If you haven't read *Crucial Conversations* or *Crucial Accountability*, I highly recommend them. They provide excellent tools for navigating hard conversations.

Additionally, seek training from HR on policies for handling difficult conversations. If you're a small business owner without formal policies, work with your local small business administration to create them.

4. Converse

The final step is to have the conversation. This is where you work toward a win-win resolution and clarify how the issue will be resolved.

First impressions matter. How you start the conversation sets a tone that can foster either

- listening or ignoring,
- calm or heightened emotions,
- ownership or defensiveness,
- resolution or further conflict.

Begin by stating the facts clearly:

- "On [date], at [time], you said __."
- "The deadline for __ was __, and your work was submitted __ days late."
- "We're here to discuss your pattern of __."

Stick to facts. Avoid inserting your feelings.

State the resolution you're aiming for. If more than one party is involved, establish norms for the conversation. Throughout, your job is to listen more than you speak. Use techniques like making eye contact, taking a few notes, and paraphrasing what the other person says to show they are seen, heard, and valued.

Stay calm—no matter what.

If an employee reacts with heightened emotions, yelling, or other big reactions, don't escalate. Stay calm, keep your tone low and steady, and focus on the facts. Losing your cool shifts the focus to your behavior instead of theirs, undermining the entire conversation.

How to End a Hard Conversation

Conflict and hard conversations can and will feel awkward for everyone involved so knowing how to end strong is a must for clarity and resolution. Make sure you follow all of your organization's specific HR policies, but below is a general idea of how to tie up hard conversations.

Clear directives: The conversation should always result in a resolution and clear action items or directives for all parties involved so that the problem, conflict, or lack of performance is resolved. All directives must have a deadline for when they must be met.

Recap: As you would do in any meeting, give a quick recap of why you met (stick to the facts), what the person shared (their rebuttal), and what directives were given (actions with deadlines).

Thank you: In hard conversations with employees, it is best to end the conversation by thanking them for stepping into the hard conversation (be sincere in this thanks).

Follow-up email: Let everyone in the room know that you will be emailing a reminder of what was discussed and the action items or directives given.

Restoration: Conflict usually leads to a negative encounter and hurt feelings. Thus, leaders need to go first in building restoration of a relationship. This could include any kind of positive interaction to counter the last negative interaction (e.g., something as simple as a smile and saying "welcome" at the next meeting).

In all situations, be sure to follow your organization's HR policies.

Documentation

The truth is, accountability conversations happen all the time. They aren't something to fear or avoid but an opportunity to navigate challenges and grow as an employee and leader. These conversations typically fall into three categories: clarification and reminders, feedback with corrective action, or releasing the poorly performing employee.

Documentation, or a record of information, is the safeguard for effective accountability.

Like securing supplies in a survival kit, documentation provides the tools needed to address challenges confidently. Verbal instructions alone are usually insufficient (e.g., this can create a "he said vs. she said" scenario). Expectations must be communicated in multiple formats—verbal, visual, and written—and reinforced regularly.

By being organized with documentation and facts, leaders are in a much better position for holding themselves and others accountable.

Documentation for Clarification of Expectations

At its core, documentation for clarity serves to establish clear expectations and provide actionable reminders. Employees need to hear, see, understand, and act upon these expectations. Regular documentation may include meeting presentations, handouts, agendas, meeting recap emails, follow-up emails, one-on-one discussions, reports, or team meetings. These steps strengthen the tent of accountability, creating a protective and clear structure where everyone knows their role and expectations.

The goal of documentation in this context is not to catch employees doing something wrong but to ensure everyone has the clarity, tools, and guidance they need to succeed. If your workplace culture feels like a constant search for mistakes, it's time to focus on rebuilding trust and relationships under the tent of accountability.

Documentation for Accountability Conversations

Inevitably, situations arise where an employee isn't meeting expectations. In these cases, documentation becomes more focused, formal, and prescriptive. Corrective feedback addresses the gap between current performance and organizational standards, offering a clear path for improvement.

After having the accountability conversation using the AC/DC method, follow up with written documentation (email, memo, evaluation software forms, etc.). This serves as the stakes that secure the tent of accountability, ensuring all parties are clear on

- the facts of the incident or pattern of behavior/performance;
- any responses or rebuttals from the employee;
- specific directives, deadlines, and resolutions.

An example follow-up email is provided to demonstrate how to effectively document an accountability conversation.

All documentation should be filed in the employee's personnel file (digital or paper). If the behavior or performance doesn't improve, the organization's HR protocols for releasing the employee should be followed.

Releasing an Employee

Unfortunately, some employees may not align with organizational expectations or culture. Even when proactive and clear expectations and training are given, poor performance can stem from a lack of motivation, ability, or insubordination. In these cases, it's the leader's responsibility to release them. Allowing a nonperforming or disruptive employee to remain poisons the team from within.

Releasing an employee isn't unkind; it's a necessary act of stewardship. It allows the individual to seek success elsewhere and protects the team that relies on a healthy and functional work environment under the tent of accountability.

Always consult your HR department to ensure proper procedures and documentation are followed before releasing an employee. By doing so, you fulfill your role as a leader who fosters accountability and builds a strong, resilient team.

> Ms. Rees,
>
> Thank you for meeting with me today about (situation, incident, lack of performance) that occurred on (date).
>
> I asked you to share what happened during the situation. Below is a brief overview:
>
> - Concise facts of her main points of explanation
> - Any important quote(s) she said that you wrote down
> - Your explanations of expectations, policies, etc.
> - Her rebuttals
> - Other relevant information in concise form
>
> As a result, you are directed to complete the following: (list specific directives for action with a hard deadline of date and time of day).
>
> I will follow up with you concerning these directives on (specific date of next meeting).
>
> Thank you,
>
> Bethany

ACCOUNTABILITY

To build a strong, resilient team, we must pack the tent of accountability in our Leadership on the Rocks survival kit and ensure that our leadership is always grounded in the structure of responsibility and clarity.

Through accountability, leaders ensure stewardship thrives and legacy endures. When built with care and purpose, accountability becomes the shelter where leaders and their teams find direction, support, and resilience to face any storm.

Apply What You've Learned

- ☐ **Workbook**: Go through this chapter's section in the Leadership on the Rocks workbook.
- ☐ **Be accountable**: You are held accountable for clarity, structure, training, and feedback concerning your employees' work, so plan how you will do the following:
  - ☐ Be clear: How will you be clear in communicating the expectations for the role?
  - ☐ Be intentional: How will you train your employees on the structure and skills needed for success?
  - ☐ Be kind: How will you structure the work and create an environment for feedback?
  - ☐ Be organized: How will you document the expectations you have given to the employee or team?
- ☐ **AC/DC conflict**: Think about an accountability conversation you need to have with a person or team. Plan it out using the AC/DC model.
- ☐ **Documentation**: Create a system and processes for documenting the behavior and work expectations you have communicated to your team members.

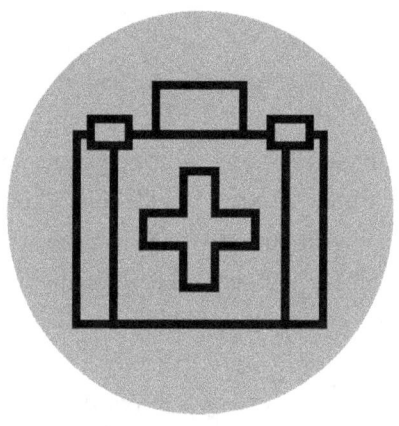

CHAPTER 13

Stewardship

The First Aid Kit

THE DAY I signed my resignation letter, I sat in tears of reflection, wondering if I had done everything in my power to care for the staff, students, and responsibilities entrusted to me in that role.

As I looked back on the situations I'd faced, I realized there were times I led well and times I fell short. Early on, I struggled with perfectionism and felt a deep sense of guilt whenever I failed to meet expectations. I wanted so badly to prove to myself that I could handle the job. Over time, I learned to embrace both successes and mistakes.

Sure, I was excited about my next adventure, but the reality of leaving the position behind brought a sobering realization: What I thought of as "mine"—my title, responsibilities, influence, the staff, and the students—was never truly mine. I had simply been stewarding them for a season.

I cared deeply and worked tirelessly, and despite my imperfections, I believe I left that position better than I found it. Leadership is messy, and no leader escapes without scars. Mistakes happen, missteps occur, and people inevitably get hurt—whether through miscommunication, unmet expectations, or unintentional neglect. That's why stewardship is like a first aid kit; it's the essential tool for addressing wounds, fostering healing, and protecting the well-being of your team and your leadership.

Just as a first aid kit is a nonnegotiable item in any survival gear, stewardship is indispensable in leadership. It requires a mindset of care, responsibility, and intentionality to repair what's broken, strengthen what's weak, and preserve what's working. A well-stocked first aid kit equips you to address injuries quickly and effectively, and stewardship ensures that you are prepared to meet the needs of your people and your mission.

The true test of stewardship comes when challenges arise. Are you prepared to pause, assess the situation, and take intentional steps to bring healing and restoration? A leader who is equipped with the first aid kit of stewardship can do just that.

What Is Stewardship?

The Leadership on the Rocks Framework defines stewardship as the act of taking care of something that belongs to someone else.

Think about it—how often do we adjust our level of effort based on who or what we believe we're working for? While some may say it's "for show," I believe the answer is deeper. It's rooted in our understanding of stewardship.

STEWARDSHIP

Too often, we claim things as "ours" when they're not. We refer to "my job," "my team," "my skills," or "my department." While these phrases aren't entirely wrong, they reflect a mindset that may need adjustment. Let's be honest—none of these things are truly ours. *We must have the courage to set aside pride and selfishness, recognizing that the positions we hold are not for self-importance or self-promotion; they are opportunities to care for others.*

Your job is not yours. It's a position of responsibility entrusted to you, and someday you'll pass it to someone else, whether due to retirement, promotion, or career changes.

Your team isn't yours either. It's a group of individuals temporarily placed under your leadership. Your role is to guide them, influence them positively, and prepare them for success, knowing that both you and they will eventually move on.

Changes happen. Transitions happen. Leadership is a season, not a lifetime guarantee. Just like players and coaches on a professional sports team, people move in and out of roles. As leaders, our time with those we serve is limited, making it all the more important to care for them well while we can. Therefore, we must have the guts to use our influence to add value to the team we lead and stand against anything that threatens it.

When we embrace a mindset of stewardship, it transforms how we lead. Stewardship fosters humility, diligence, and courage to care deeply for others and approach leadership with integrity.

Key Takeaway:

Leaders use their influence to serve the things, situations, and people placed within their care.

The Basics of Stewardship

Stewardship isn't just a mindset; it's also a skill set. As stewards, we must be intentional in three key areas: assessing, investing, and being accountable. These practical steps are essential in tending to the people, teams, and projects under our care.

1. Assess

The first step in being a good steward is to assess what you've been given. To assess means to evaluate the nature, value, or quality of something. This is where we look for facts that give us a clearer picture of the situation, including what's going well and what needs attention:

- *Take account.* Often, our roles and responsibilities aren't clearly defined. This can lead to confusion, especially when expectations haven't been communicated. This lack of clarity can cause problems, and the blame game often follows. Don't let assumptions or misunderstandings about your responsibilities lead to failure. When stepping into a leadership role, have the guts to seek clarity on what you are responsible for, whether that's personnel, budgets, policies, or specific tasks. Be proactive in understanding your role and asking about key areas of responsibility, such as
  - personnel management (hiring, firing, evaluations);
  - budgets and financial oversight;
  - projects, goals, and workflows;
  - policies and initiatives;
  - customer service and stakeholder relationships; or
  - building operations.

The stakes are high, especially when it comes to people and finances. I've heard it said that the two things that will get you fired or send you to jail are the mistreating of personnel or the mishandling of the budget. If you are new to the concept of stewardship, I suggest you prioritize learning about how to take care of your people and the budget. If you're unsure about how to manage these areas, take time to meet with HR and finance departments to understand the expectations.

- *Find the good.* It's easy to focus on the problems and challenges, but it's important to also recognize what's going well. Many of us naturally focus on the negatives, but this mindset can prevent us from seeing the blessings and strengths around us. When assessing a situation, team, or project, begin by looking for the positive aspects. This shift in perspective can help you approach challenges with greater hope and motivation, leading to better outcomes.
- *Find the gaps.* After assessing for strengths, it's time to identify where things fall short. This involves looking at the gaps between where you are and where you want to be. Use this process to gain clarity on what steps need to be taken to improve. Finding these gaps isn't about criticism; it's about discovering opportunities for growth. Once you've identified the gaps, prioritize which ones to address first to make meaningful progress.

2. Invest

The second key area of stewardship is investing. To invest means providing the necessary resources for growth. These resources could include time, attention, support, coaching, tools, and money. Growth doesn't happen automatically just because you invest resources; it requires thoughtful, strategic action.

Too often leaders assume that activity equals progress, but busyness doesn't necessarily lead to results. If you want your team to grow and succeed, you must be intentional with how you invest in them. For example, investing in your own personal growth as a leader, as well as supporting the growth of your team, is crucial. Great employees will not stay where they are without support or development for future opportunities. Without this intentional investment, growth won't happen naturally.

If we are to be good stewards of what is entrusted to our leadership, then we need to invest the resources needed to produce personal and team growth. What you invest in today affects your tomorrow. How are you investing in leadership development for yourself and your people?

3. Be Accountable
The third and final step in stewardship is accountability. Accountability means taking responsibility for the outcomes of your leadership. It's easy to want quick fixes or shortcuts, but lasting results require patience.

Those types of programs or fixes don't make long-lasting changes because they don't change or grow the beliefs, behaviors, or actions behind the problems in the first place. Long-lasting results will always need time to grow and cultivate. Stewardship is about recognizing the bigger picture and being committed to long-term progress.

As a leader, you must stay focused on your mission, even when facing setbacks like market fluctuations or personnel challenges. True progress comes from consistent, steady effort, not from chasing quick solutions. Progress is made through consistent, deliberate action, one step at a time.

Accountability also means acknowledging both successes and failures. When things go well, give credit to those involved. When things don't go as planned, take ownership and identify how to improve. As a steward, you are responsible for ensuring the growth and progress of your team.

Effective stewardship as a leader requires the practical steps of assessing what you've been given, investing the necessary resources for growth, and being accountable for the outcomes of your actions. These three areas are essential for ensuring steady progress and long-term success.

High Will/High Skill

As leaders, we must ensure that our team members are not just functioning but thriving. That means whether it's a current employee or an applicant, we must be able to assess their overall motivation and abilities. The High Will/High Skill chart is a tool that helps us do just that—assess where each team member stands in terms of motivation (will) and ability (skill) and provide the necessary care to help them perform at their best.

This chart is one of my favorite tools for creating and maintaining a healthy team. This visual tool helps define the beliefs and behaviors needed for success in a role, while also identifying the "parasites"—those negative beliefs and behaviors—that need to be addressed to preserve the team's health.

I use this chart to assess applicants before I hire them and as a benchmark for giving feedback for growth.

Defining Desired Beliefs and Behaviors

Before using the High Will/High Skill chart, it's crucial to assess the beliefs and behaviors of top-performing employees. Leaders need to evaluate and define what attitudes and behaviors make someone effective in their role and hire accordingly. This involves being intentional in understanding what "health" looks like in your team.

Once you hire someone, you are now responsible for their development—addressing any beliefs or behaviors (good or bad) that they exhibit.

Here are examples of beliefs you want to see in your team members. These act as foundational principles for good health:

- Concerning *themselves*, do they possess a growth/abundance mindset that allows them to learn from challenges and bounce back from setbacks?
- Concerning *others*, do they value fostering positive relationships?
- Regarding their *work*, do they value quality, efficiency, and striving for excellence in their job?
- Regarding *change*, are they flexible and able to think critically to solve problems and adapt to new challenges?

These beliefs act as vital signs of a healthy mindset, but behaviors are just as important as beliefs. These are not merely personality traits but heart-driven actions that demonstrate the capacity for growth and impact. As a leader, it's essential to recognize the behaviors that indicate someone has the heart strength to thrive in their role. For example, consider how high-performing individuals behave in each of these roles:

- As *employees*, what actions do they take to contribute to tangible, measurable results in their role?
- As *colleagues*, how do they foster collaboration and strengthen teamwork?
- As *leaders*, what behaviors help them positively influence and inspire others?
- As *service providers*, do they consistently act in the best interests of all stakeholders?

Good stewards don't hire blindly. They outline the desired and the not-so-desired beliefs and behaviors needed to be successful on the team or in the organization. They become crystal clear about the beliefs and behaviors they expect to hire and grow on their team.

By working through this beliefs and behaviors checklist, you will be able to identify what a top-performing employee exhibits. Likewise, you can answer these questions in a negative context by identifying what a poorly performing employee exhibits. You'll use the identified positive and negative beliefs and behaviors when you create the High Will/High Skill chart.

Building a High Will/High Skill Chart

Now that you've clarified the desired beliefs and behaviors, it's time to create the High Will/High Skill chart. This one-page tool helps you categorize employees into four quadrants, making it easier to determine where they stand concerning motivation and skill and how to proceed. Here are the four quadrants.

1. **Low Will/Low Skill:** These individuals have neither the motivation nor the ability to perform well in their roles. They represent that *insubordinate* employee who does not perform their job. Avoid hiring or retaining employees in this quadrant, as their negativity will harm the team's overall health and morale. They are like contagious diseases that if left untreated will infect the rest of the team.
2. **Low Will/High Skill:** These employees have the skill but lack the motivation to apply it. They represent the *disgruntled* employee who teeters on the line of doing the job but makes everyone miserable in the process. This situation can cause the most frustration because they have the potential but choose not to use it. It's vital to intervene quickly through encouragement and coaching. If they are allowed to linger in this quadrant too long, they will cause your high-potential and top-performing employees to leave.

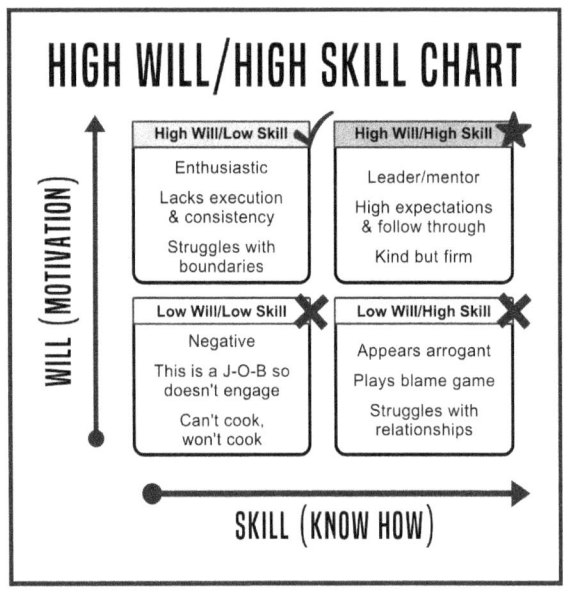

3. **High Will/Low Skill:** This is where most *new hires* begin. They have the motivation to succeed but lack the skills to do so. These employees are often eager to learn and can be easily coached. However, if left too long without developing their skills, they may become stuck and frustrated. It's crucial to provide training and support so they can build the skills they need to perform successfully. If employees stay in this quadrant too long, they will cause you the most heartache because they're so nice, but they're just not producing the results needed.
4. **High Will/High Skill:** These are your *high potential, top performers*. They are motivated and skilled, making them invaluable to the team. These employees are critical to long-term success and are the ones who will help guide the rest of the team forward. The employees in this quadrant make up the pipeline for your future leaders and will bring you the most inspiration.

The Goal of Stewardship

The ultimate goal of stewardship is that when a team is entrusted to you, it's your job to help each person move toward the High Will/High Skill quadrant. When hiring new employees, be intentional in hiring those who exhibit strong will, as it's easier to teach skills than to change someone's mindset. However, to those industries that must have high skill employees (surgeons, engineers, etc.), be intentional in coaching for high will.

However, it's important to remember that most high will/high skill employees won't tolerate working with low-performing team members who negatively impact the culture and draw the same paycheck as they do. As a leader, be ready to address those situations quickly and decisively.

The Role of the High Will/High Skill Chart in Stewardship

Good stewards don't have their employees guessing at the beliefs and behaviors needed to be successful on the team and promote health to the organization. The High Will/High Skill chart is a useful tool for addressing immediate needs, providing clarity, and helping guide performance. It allows you to intentionally take these actions:

- *Clarify expectations.* Employees know what's expected of them and where they stand.
- *Set goals.* Provides a framework for professional growth.
- *Give feedback.* Offers a clear structure for coaching and corrective actions.

By creating and using this chart regularly, you'll minimize excuses and miscommunication, allowing you to hold team members accountable for their performance. When everyone is clear about expectations and knows how to grow and improve, the entire team can thrive.

Good stewardship isn't just about hiring the right people; it's about cultivating an environment where everyone can grow and perform at their best. By using first aid tools like the High Will/High Skill chart, you'll be able to treat the root causes of poor performance and guide your team toward long-term success.

Stewardship is about recognizing that what we often call "ours"—our talents, teams, projects, and roles—are not truly ours to possess. They are gifts entrusted to us, and our responsibility is to nurture, enhance, and elevate them so they are stronger and more impactful than before.

STEWARDSHIP

As leaders, we are stewards of the people and resources we lead, tasked with promoting their growth and productivity.

Our role as stewards is to add value by improving the health and performance of what's entrusted to us. This requires us to be proactive in addressing unhealthy beliefs and behaviors and ensuring that our teams have what they need to succeed. Stewardship is not passive; it requires action. And that action often involves the guts of leadership—the courage to step in and provide the first aid needed when beliefs or behaviors become misaligned. Just as we pack first aid in our Leadership on the Rocks survival kit to address wounds, we must be ready to provide the corrective care that will help our teams thrive and continue to grow.

By promoting the health of what we lead and taking responsibility for addressing any wounds or weaknesses, we build a strong foundation that will endure long after we've passed on the torch.

Apply What You've Learned

- ☐ **Workbook**: Go through this chapter's section in the Leadership on the Rocks workbook.
- ☐ **Assess**: Analyze the scope of your work and the skill sets of your team and establish your priorities. Celebrate the good. Identify the gaps between where your work/team is and where it needs to be.
- ☐ **Invest**: Decide what resources and support you need to provide your team for professional growth and to increase their efficiency and effectiveness.
- ☐ **Be accountable**: Create a plan to take the "next right step" to add value to all stakeholders so that progress is made. Give credit to others for what is working well and take ownership of what is not working well.

- ☐ **Beliefs and behaviors checklist**: Create two avatar employee types: top performer with high potential and low performer who needs to be released. Create a checklist of the beliefs and behaviors each of those employee types would have.
- ☐ **High Will/High Skill chart**: Using the beliefs and behaviors checklist, create a high will/high skill chart that clarifies employee expectations. You can use this chart to hire and grow your employees.

CHAPTER 14

Legacy

The Survival Manual to Pass On

I'VE ALWAYS HAD a heart to encourage and coach those just a step behind me in life and leadership. It's not that I think I have it all figured out and want to give advice. In fact, when sharing my experiences, I often say, "Here's what happened and what I learned from it—trash or treasure." The purpose behind this sharing isn't to give advice. When solicited or appropriate for the situation, sharing can provide others with encouragement, insight, and wisdom: encouragement to remind them that their current season is temporary, insight as to what possibilities lie ahead, and wisdom to help them avoid the same bumps and bruises I've already encountered.

How we treat others, how we walk with them, and how we help them grow in life and leadership will ultimately build our legacy. Picture this: What if instead of feeling lost in a valley of despair, the emerging leaders around us saw us waving at them, showing them a way to higher ground?

Surviving the harsh terrain is one thing; thriving in it is another. The key difference is preparation—and this is where our leadership legacy comes in. Legacy is the survival manual of leadership that we write and pack in the Leadership on the Rocks survival kits of others.

When we focus on building a positive legacy, we create a practical, intentional guide that ensures our influence and impact extend far beyond our time in the role. It's the path we forge through our values, our choices, and our actions, empowering others to find their way to success.

As John Maxwell puts it, "It takes a leader to know a leader, grow a leader, and show a leader."[41] Legacy isn't something you leave behind by accident—it's something you build on purpose. Every choice you make, every person you mentor, every system you implement is shaping the leadership you leave behind. It's about preparing others, guiding them, and ensuring they too have their own survival manual to navigate the challenges ahead.

The Leadership on the Rocks Framework defines legacy as the long-lasting impact we have on those around us.

It's not about focusing inward on our own leadership but about looking outward—being intentional with how we influence, teach, and build others up. It's about giving them the tools, the wisdom, and the capacity to nourish and protect their own leadership body. And just like we build for ourselves the Leadership on the Rocks survival kit we've discussed, we must help those who follow us craft their own survival kit, fully equipped to lead in their own way.

As leaders, we have an obligation to pour out our knowledge, wisdom, and encouragement, mentoring the next generation of leaders.

The team or organization you lead is not yours to keep; one day, someone else will step into your role.

The more leadership development opportunities organizations provide for their employees, the more their employees will want to stay within that organization. Believe it or not, those emerging leaders will even start recruiting other emerging leaders to join them. A culture that grows individuals as leaders and prepares them for the next step in their career sounds like an organization most professionals want to work for.

The unfortunate reality is that organizations will give you the title, the team, and the to-do list, but they won't necessarily equip you to lead. Bosses and organizations are notorious for empowering people to go forth and "do the thing," without ever actually equipping employees in how to "do the thing." They can expect people to automatically "know what they know" and "think what they think" when it comes to being a leader.

Assuming that being a high functioning, individual contributor equates to being prepared for the challenges of leadership is a fallacy. Without proper mentoring, modeling, and coaching, these individuals can feel overwhelmed and unsupported. They may end up stepping into leadership roles with no clear direction, facing an avalanche of challenges that lead them to burn out, become cynical, or even retreat from leadership altogether.

Failing to equip leaders is a leadership failure that organizations must address immediately. Leadership development should never be an afterthought; it should be a core part of an organization's culture. But as we know, many organizations neglect to invest in leadership training, mentorship, and coaching. The responsibility often falls on individual leaders to build their own leadership pipelines, to guide others, and to develop the next generation of leaders who are ready to step up.

Good stewards design intentional paths for emerging leaders, ensuring these individuals are equipped to lead and serve when the opportunity arises. The most important part of your leadership legacy within an organization is not what employees do when you're around but what they do when you're not.

True leaders create lasting impact by building leadership capacity in others—helping them improve their skills, shaping their mindset, and giving them the opportunities they need to apply what they've learned.

Think about it:

- How many individual contributors struggle to mitigate problems proactively because they've never been explicitly taught leadership principles?
- How many people are promoted without ever having had a mentor to model quality leadership?
- How many newly promoted leaders are left to figure things out on their own with no coaching to guide them through the conflicts and challenges ahead?

Key Takeaway:

Great leaders are intentional in teaching, modeling, and coaching others using the Leadership on the Rocks Framework.

Individual contributors can grow into exceptional leaders, but they need guidance and support. Just as we pack our own Leadership on the Rocks survival kit, we must help others pack theirs so they are prepared to face whatever comes next.

Creating a survival manual for legacy is about being intentional in building a leader mentorship program. It's about setting up systems that equip the next generation of leaders with the tools and insights they'll need to thrive. Let's dive into the *how* of building a legacy by developing emerging leaders.

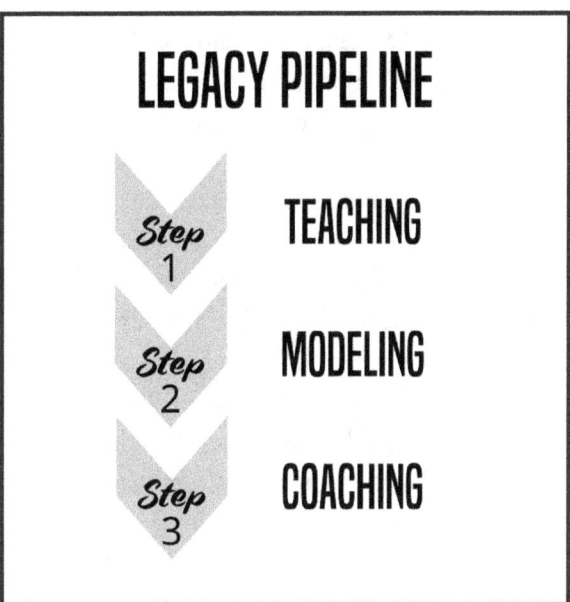

1. Teaching

Great leadership doesn't just occur; it is cultivated and developed, much like how the body grows stronger over time with intentional action. Just like people can't read minds and thus need explicit instructions, emerging leaders don't automatically know what seasoned leaders know. Osmosis (automatic assimilation) never works, and inaction never accomplishes anything. As my husband says, "We should always be bent towards action."

The first action to take in developing emerging leaders is to teach them about leadership. Quality teaching provides what they need (skills) when they need it (readiness level) so they can take the next step forward (growth and progress). Teaching is not handing them a leadership book and sending them on their way, giving yourself credit for providing professional growth.

We know we should be intentional in growing leaders, but "should" is not a commitment to action. As James Bishop, a wise relative of mine, says: "The phrase 'I need to…' or 'I should…' is not a goal or a commitment. Before you know it, you're 'shoulding' all over yourself."

Schedule your priorities because other things will always creep in and steal your good intentions. You must schedule time to teach emerging leaders about leadership. If you don't schedule it, it will never happen.

Don't overthink the scheduling either. Quality teaching happens best in five-to-fifteen-minute spurts. Our brains need time to process new information so it can be connected to what we already know. Without time to process, the new information won't stick in our long-term memory. That is why an all-day training exhausts the brain and people can only remember a few tidbits from it.

Look to schedule moments (not hours or days) to explicitly teach about the Leadership on the Rocks Framework. It can be simple to embed teaching leadership into what you are already doing. For example, schedule five minutes in your meeting agenda to have a leadership teaching point with a personal story of how you learned that lesson. When talking with a team about a problem they're working to solve, explicitly teach a leadership principle that will help them in their work (e.g., how to assess root causes, how to build a collaborative team, how to get buy-in). When talking with individual team members about their professional growth goals, connect them with leadership courses and mentors in those areas. Then schedule follow-up conversations with them to discuss what they are learning and how they are applying it.

If growing emerging leaders or building a pipeline of future leaders is a priority, then schedule the time to explicitly teach best leadership practices. When time is made for explicitly teaching leadership, it raises the leadership lid of every individual contributor on your team. The more time you invest in teaching, the more the body of leadership within your organization grows.

2. Modeling

The second action to take in developing emerging leaders is to model quality leadership. To model is to show what something looks like when it is in use. Use the old cliches: "Practice what you preach" because "more is caught than taught!" You are always on display, modeling what leadership looks like.

We're not talking about modeling clothing here, but how leaders have integrity;

- continue to learn and grow in their leadership;
- build relationships with all people and stakeholders;
- prioritize goals;
- clearly communicate so people know, understand, and can take action;
- respond in times of crisis or chaos;
- intentionally plan for the future;
- mitigate problems from happening again; and
- have hard conversations that resolve conflict and hold everyone accountable.

One of my biggest pet peeves is watching a hypocrite in action. Internally, I feel furious when people mouth off about expectations of others that they don't meet themselves. Don't get me wrong; nobody is perfect, but leaders are called to live above reproach (free from habits and behaviors that would impede setting the highest standard and model).

People can quickly and easily spot a hypocrite. As a leader, your actions are always being watched, and you are setting the norm for what is allowed, encouraged, and rewarded. Leaders need to be giving grace to their employees, not asking for it. Leaders, don't put yourself in a position to need to ask for forgiveness for being late, missing a meeting you scheduled, not communicating well, losing your temper, or not having integrity. When your employees have to constantly give you grace, you are exhausting them, not growing them as leaders.

Be intentional in what you model. Walk/talk people through the situation you are experiencing by sharing what you are thinking, best practices you are leaning on, decisions you are weighing, and if applicable, what mentors you are reaching out to. This time of modeling will also allow for deeper relationship building because you are being vulnerable in sharing your own growth as a leader. You're giving them a front row seat into what personal accountability looks like and how it is required to grow through mistakes and triumphs alike.

3. Coaching

The third action to take in developing emerging leaders is to coach for quality leadership. Coaching has already been mentioned several times throughout this book because it is imperative to being a leader who serves and grows others as leaders.

Coaches help people walk through scenarios and situations they've already experienced or will experience in real-life leadership. However, a coaching partnership doesn't just happen. It must be cultivated.

I was an instructional coach in an educational setting for almost a decade. As I worked to create coaching partnerships with teachers, there were four phases we would walk through in our coaching cycle. As I transitioned into leadership coaching, I continued using these principles because they are universal, and they work. These are four phases for coaching:

1. Building relationships (establishing trust)
2. Equipping with skills (focusing on their goals and learning)

3. Empowering with purpose (creating opportunities to practice)
4. Making an impact (providing mentorship)

These phases should not come as a shock to you because building relationships to better equip and empower others to make an impact is at the heart of all the leadership tools we've discussed. Here I'll expand upon those concepts to explain how they apply in a coaching partnership.

Building Relationships (Establishing Trust)

Just like with a team, a positive relationship built on trust is the foundation of any coaching partnership and must be the priority. The reason building trust is the first phase is because vulnerability is required for growth to happen. Employees will not be vulnerable with people they don't like or trust.

It's important to note that it is often difficult for the "boss" to be the coach because employees don't typically want to be vulnerable about any weakness to the person who fills out their evaluation paperwork. For this reason, coaching usually needs to come from a third party so that an honest conversation won't be seen as a threat to their performance evaluation, fodder for gossip, or a reflection on their overall value as a person and professional.

Equipping with Skills (Focusing on Their Goals and Learning)

After a relationship of trust is established, a coach needs to focus on growing the knowledge and skills of the employee, but not by giving advice. Instead ask more reflective questions, allowing the participant to make their own choices.

Coaching is what exponentially produces individual growth in employees because it focuses on what they need most. Coaches ask questions that invite sharing:

- What would you like to talk about today?
- What's something you've been thinking about or working through recently?
- What are your leadership goals?
- What are you already doing to grow as a leader?
- What is one leadership area you want to concentrate on to make the biggest impact?
- How can I best support you right now?

Once one goal is chosen by the emerging leader, the coach helps the employee become equipped with the skills they need to be successful in that area. Coaches don't tell emerging leaders what to do because they focus on helping them build the muscles of thinking and problem-solving skills. Thus the goal is to ensure they understand how to utilize the leadership "tools" and recognize what tool is needed in their current situation.

Empowering with Purpose (Creating Opportunities to Practice)

Once trust is established and emerging leaders gain some of the skills needed, it's time to apply those skills in practice. Just as the guts of leadership help guide accountability, the practice phase empowers emerging leaders to put what they've learned into action.

The practice could take many forms:

- Share a current problem/project/situation they are working on. For example, package the information of a project to give or send briefs to stakeholders.
- Plan for a future event or project, such as strategizing how to get buy-in for a new initiative.
- Respond to a mock scenario. For instance, role-play mediating a conflict or managing a challenging conversation.

While the emerging leader is working on or talking through their approach to the situation or scenario, the coach engages in a structured support process by

1. observing (listens and watches leaders in action),
2. taking notes (records observations for immediate one-on-one feedback),
3. asking reflective questions (encourages the leader to think critically about their performance),
4. providing feedback (shares a few tidbits of positive and constructive feedback, ensuring it's actionable and not overwhelming),
5. strategizing (helps the leader develop a game plan for improved performance).

It's essential for coaches to avoid overwhelming the emerging leader with a long list of corrections. Often, the leader already senses what needs improvement but may be unsure of the next step. Instead of providing all the answers, coaches focus on asking great reflective questions throughout the process. This approach encourages emerging leaders to process and reflect on their own performance, fostering growth and independence.

Key reflection covers areas like these:

- What went well?
- What didn't go well?
- What could have been done differently to make it better (lessons learned)?
- What resource or skill is needed to be more successful?
- What is the next step of action?

By guiding leaders to analyze their experiences and take deliberate steps forward, coaches empower them to grow and excel in their leadership journey.

Making an Impact (Providing Mentorship)

After coaching, the employee will have emerged as a leader ready for a role of increased authority and influence. Once the emerging leader is equipped with the skills they need, the coach's role shifts to that of a mentor. They become the trusted advisor who checks in with them, discusses their specific pain points or current situations, and provides guidance. This is where the relationship deepens, and the legacy of leadership takes shape.

Everyone needs a mentor—someone to call when they are faced with tough decisions. Even CEOs need other CEOs for guidance and support. Similarly, we all need someone to help us make an impact with the skills and leadership legacy we've developed.

As mentors, we help emerging leaders refine their leadership philosophy and approach. Just like a survival manual, mentorship offers the guidance needed to navigate through leadership challenges with a steady hand.

As we reach the summit of our leadership journey together, it's clear that the survival manual is more than just a tool in your Leadership on the Rocks survival kit—it's the cornerstone of your legacy. Legacy is not just the lasting impact you leave behind; it's the way you intentionally pour into others, shaping their skills, sharpening their thinking, and preparing them for opportunities yet to come.

Great leaders don't hoard their wisdom or influence—they share it. They invest in building leadership capacity in others, creating a ripple effect that strengthens individuals, teams, and organizations. By equipping and empowering emerging leaders to rise to their own challenges, you're crafting a pipeline of talent and visionaries ready to continue the work you've started.

When stewardship and legacy converge, accountability evolves into something far greater. It becomes the thriving, secure environment where growth flourishes, challenges are met with confidence, and resilience becomes second nature. Equipped with the tools to mend what's broken and chart a path forward, you'll not only lead effectively but build something that endures—even when leadership feels "on the rocks."

So as you prepare to pass the torch, remember to pull out your survival manual. Use it to document the lessons learned, the principles that shaped your leadership, and the strategies that helped you and your team navigate the terrain. Then pass it on.

Your legacy isn't just what you leave behind—it's how you inspire others to lead with purpose, strength, and resilience. The time to start writing your manual is now. And the time to empower others to write theirs is always.

Apply What You've Learned

- ☐ **Workbook**: Go through this chapter's section in the Leadership on the Rocks workbook.
- ☐ **Teach**: Schedule and embed leadership development into the workday.

- **Model**: People imitate what they see, and "more is caught than taught." Reflect on the behaviors you are modeling. Remember, don't mandate it if you can't model it.
- **Coach**: Create a plan to develop emerging leaders by providing opportunities for coaching.
    - Building relationships: Build trust with those you are coaching. Be vulnerable, transparent, and focused on the individual you are coaching. Keep all coaching matters confidential.
    - Equipping with skills: Do not give advice, but ask open-ended and reflective questions to give them the opportunity to think through situations and analyze from a leader perspective.
    - Empowering with purpose: Create opportunities for emerging leaders to practice and implement their leadership skills (e.g., planning, organizing, and rolling out special projects, presentations, events).
    - Making an impact: Be a mentor. Develop a mentor relationship with a new leader.

EPILOGUE

THRIVING ON THE ROCKS

LEADERSHIP "ON THE ROCKS" doesn't have to mean failure or frustration. With the right mindset, tools, and intentional effort, the very rocks that once tripped you up can become the foundation for a legacy of resilience and impact. By using the Leadership on the Rocks survival kit, you've not only learned to survive the harsh terrain of leadership but to thrive in it.

At the start of this journey, leadership might have felt like a landslide—an overwhelming cascade of problems, conflicts, and constraints that left you stranded in a valley of despair. But step by step, tool by tool, you've learned to climb out of that valley and build a leadership foundation that can weather any storm.

The process hasn't been about finding perfection or following a rigid map. Instead, it's been about progress—about equipping your head, heart, hands, and guts with the tools necessary to lead with confidence, clarity, and purpose. You've turned obstacles into stepping stones, setbacks into opportunities, and moments of chaos into catalysts for growth.

This book has been more than just a guide; it's been a call to action. The survival kit you've packed is now yours to use as you continue to build, strengthen, and sustain your leadership. Whether it's the compass of identity and map of purpose guiding your direction, the match of service sparking action, or the tent of accountability creating a safe space for growth, you have everything you need to navigate the ever-changing landscape of leadership.

But survival isn't the final goal—thriving is. Thriving means embracing the process of progress, not perfection. It means recognizing that leadership is less about reaching a destination and more about becoming the kind of leader who can adapt, grow, and inspire others along the way. It's about using the lessons you've learned to build something enduring—not just for yourself but for those you lead.

As you move forward, remember that your leadership journey doesn't end here. The tools in your survival kit are meant to be used, refined, and shared. Your survival manual is still being written—not just for your benefit but for the emerging leaders who will one day follow in your footsteps.

So take the next step. Prioritize your pain points, tackle challenges with intention, and continue building your leadership on the rocks—the essential rocks. And as you do, know that you're not just surviving; you're thriving, creating a legacy of resilience, strength, and purpose that will outlast any storm.

Thank you for allowing me to be part of your journey. If you ever need additional support, whether through leadership courses, coaching, or training, know that my company, BR Essential Services, is here to help. Visit us at www.leadershipontherocks.com to learn more.

Until we meet again, keep climbing, keep building, and keep thriving on the rocks—the essential rocks.

Don't forget to go to www.leadershipontherocks.com/freeworkbook and download your free Leadership on the Rocks workbook to help you in each area we've covered in the book.

ACKNOWLEDGEMENTS

THE CONCEPT FOR this book was built on a lifetime of personal experiences where God faithfully guided my path—deepening my trust in Him, shaping my understanding, and ultimately softening my heart to see His leadership through the wilderness of my own. Every step, every stumble, every summit—He was there. Thank you, Jesus, for being the ultimate leader of my life. Without You, this testimony of surviving, adapting, and succeeding would not exist. My leadership would be empty...a chasing after the wind.

To my wonderfully supportive, wise, fun-loving, and sarcastic family—Jason, Austin, and Ashlyn—thank you for being my safe space and my comedy club. For every "30 seconds of awkwardness with Mom" I delivered in the name of leadership, you've given me ten more lessons about humility, love, taking myself less seriously... and that not everything needs a strategy—sometimes, you just need a good crawfish boil. You are my joy on this side of heaven.

To every student, educator, parent, school, and community I've served over the past two decades—thank you. You were my training ground, my test lab, and my inspiration. I didn't always get it right, but walking the road with you has made me better. And to my "ride-or-die" fellow educators and administrators: Thank you for the laughs, lessons, and limps. I'd go to battle with you any day—just as long as there's coffee and a functioning copier.

To my brother Jon-Perry—thank you for reading this book in its original, "bless her heart" form and offering your editorial magic (and patience) to help shape it into what it is today. You made it readable *and* respectable.

To my amazing family—Mom, Dad, Joseph, Tyler, Lori, Rebecca, Courtney, Mike, Debbie, Ambur, Mandy, Brandon, and Donnie—thank you for your feedback, your endless encouragement, and your heroic endurance of my text threads filled with questions about colors, layouts, and whether a compass or a map metaphor made more sense. Your support—and your design style eye—was everything.

To Janice Thompson, thank you for saying "yes" to God and hosting a church small group for wannabe authors. Without your leadership and the safe space you created, this book would still be stuck in my head, half-formed and untitled—or maybe mentally filed away under *"Maybe Someday."*

To Rachel D. Baker and my tribe of friends, fellow authors, podcasters, bloggers, coaches, and entrepreneurs—thank you for being a lighthouse of encouragement and proof that the creative world is big enough for all of us. There's no competition here, only a rising tide lifting all boats (and books).

To Chloie, my incredible book project manager—thank you for walking me through "all the things" of publishing. I promise I didn't mean to send *that many* emails (okay, maybe I did). Your calm in my chaos was a gift.

To Traci Matt, my developmental editor—you matched my humor and helped shape my chaos of metaphors into one cohesive narrative. Thank you for not letting me wander too far into the wilderness without a map—or at least a good punchline.

ACKNOWLEDGEMENTS

To Cindy Venable, my copy editor—thank you for your grammar superpowers and gentle red pen. Without you, my sentence structure would've been... let's just say "adventurous."

To Will and Alex at Streamline—this book is a result of your vision, your faith, and your commitment to helping authors make a *Hidden Impact*™. Thank you for building an environment where stories are honored and stewarded with excellence. Your obedience to God's call has changed lives—starting with mine.

And finally, to the reader holding this book: thank you for opening these pages. Whether you're climbing the leadership mountain, stuck in the valley, or somewhere on the rocky trail—this book was written for you. Keep going. You're not alone. And you've got more strength (and tools) than you realize.

ENDNOTES

All Scripture quotations are from the Holy Bible, English Standard Version (ESV®), copyright © 2001 by Crossway Bibles, a publishing ministry of Good News Publishers. Used by permission. All rights reserved.

1 Stephen R. Covey, *The 7 Habits of Highly Effective People: Restoring the Character Ethic* (Simon and Schuster,1989).
2 Gary Klein, "Mindsets: What They Are and Why They Matter," *Psychology Today*, May 1, 2016, https://www.psychologytoday.com/us/blog/seeing-what-others-dont/201605/mindsets.
3 Carol Dweck, *Mindset: The New Psychology of Success* (Random House, 2006).
4 Covey, Stephen. *7 Habits of Highly Effective People*. 1989.
5 Michelle Spadafora, guest, *Leadership on the Rocks*, podcast, episode 45, "Stewardship and Health with Michelle Spadafora," July 26, 2023, https://open.spotify.com/episode/51t9r9dHEAnoG6A7Mu9EoO?si=AG05grlDS6KiskKMMmNdwA.
6 Daniel Goleman, *Emotional Intelligence: Why It Can Matter More Than IQ* (Bantam Books, 1995).
7 Allison Aars (@thefestivefarmhouse), Instagram, November 3, 2018, https://www.instagram.com/p/BpuL7AWng_H/?epik=dj0yJnU9Z05BWVFybEloTEFuUUFjMjBBbGFuSmxicXQyekY4dEsmcD0wJm49enJaM0pYdXBWTmhzU2daMi00UTF4USZ0PUFBQUFBR1U3X3lN.

8   Craig Groeschel, *The Power to Change: Mastering the Habits That Matter Most* (Zondervan Books. 2023).
9   View the video series at https://freedom.churchofthehighlands.com/curriculum.
10 Michael Gerber, *The E Myth Revisited: Why Most Small Businesses Don't Work and What to Do About It* (Harper Collins, 1995),139.
11 To learn more about these people who live in Blue Zones, see https://www.bluezones.com/explorations/okinawa-japan/.
12 Simon Sinek, *Start with Why: How Great Leaders Inspire Everyone to Take Action* (Penguin, 2009), 50.
13 Ken Blanchard et al., *Lead Like Jesus Revisited: Lessons from the Greatest Leadership Role Model of All Time* (W Publishing, 2016), 144.
14 To read about Chick-Fil-A's purpose and culture, see https://www.chick-fil-a.com/careers/culture.
15 To learn more about the work of the Alzheimer's Association, see https://www.alz.org/about.
16 John Maxwell, *The 21 Irrefutable Laws of Leadership* (HarperCollins Leadership, 2007), 267.
17 "How to Hire Employees: The 12 Components to a Good Hire," Ramsey Solutions, August 23, 2023, https://www.ramseysolutions.com/business/how-to-hire-employees.
18 Saul McLeod, PhD, "Maslow's Hierarchy of Needs," Simply Psychology, updated April 4, 2022, https://www.simplypsychology.org/maslow.html.
19 Brené Brown, *Dare to Lead: Brave Work. Tough Conversations. Whole Hearts.* (Random House, 2018), 70.
20 "Culture Eats Strategy for Breakfast," Quote Investigator, May 23, 2017, https://quoteinvestigator.com/2017/05/23/culture-eats/.
21 Seth Godin, *This is Marketing: You Can't Be Seen Until You Learn to See* (Penguin, 2018), 102.
22 Jon Gordon, *The Energy Bus: 10 Rules to Fuel Your Life, Work, and Team with Positive Energy* (John Wiley & Sons, 2007).
23 Simon Sinek, *Leaders Eat Last: Why Some Teams Pull Together and Others Don't* (Portfolio, 2014), 29.

ENDNOTES

24 Kerry Patterson et al., *Crucial Conversations: Tools for Talking When Stakes Are High* (McGraw-Hill Education, 2012).

25 Andy Stanley (@AndyStanley), "Leaders who refuse to listen will eventually be surrounded by people who have nothing significant to say," Twitter, August 17, 2011, https://twitter.com/AndyStanley/status/103841035108630528.

26 Joseph McCormack, *Brief: Make a Bigger Impact by Saying Less* (John Wiley & Sons, 2014).

27 The DISC Personality Profile is a proprietary tool developed based on the DISC theory of psychologist William Moulton Marston. The version discussed in this book is derived from the John Maxwell DISC Method, part of the Maxwell Leadership Certified Team training program. For more information, visit https://www.leadershipontherocks.com/DISC.

28 Bruce W. Tuckman and Mary Ann C. Jensen, "Stages of Small-Group Development Revisited," *Group & Organization Studies* 2, no. 4 (1977): 419–427, https://doi.org/10.1177/105960117700200404.

29 Patrick Lencioni, *The Five Dysfunctions of a Team* (Jossey-Bass, 2002).

30 Greg McKeown, *Essentialism: The Disciplined Pursuit of Less* (Crown Business, 2014).

31 Jim Collins, *Good to Great: Why Some Companies Make the Leap… and Others Don't* (Random House Business Books, 2001).

32 Dwight D. Eisenhower, "Remarks at the National Defense Executive Reserve Conference" Nov. 14, 1957, Pub. Papers, No. 235, Fed. Reg., 818.

33 Greg McKeown, *Effortless: Make It Easier to Do What Matters Most* (Currency, 2021), 27.

34 Michael Hyatt, *Free to Focus: A Total Productivity System to Achieve More by Doing Less* (Baker Book, a division of Baker Publishing Group, 2019), 89.

35 Colin Baker, "9 Leadership Roles to Know in Business," Leaders Media, June 10, 2022, leaders.com/articles/leadership/leadership-roles/.

36 Charles R. Swindoll, *Life Is 10% What Happens to You and 90% How You React: Cultivating Inner Strength and Embracing Hope When Life is Not What You Expected* (Thomas Nelson, 2023).

37 This is not a quote by Dr. King but more of a paraphrase from a sermon he gave the day after Bloody Sunday in Selma, Alabama on March 8, 1965. Speech script at https://faculty.etsu.edu/history/documents/mlkselma.htm.

38 Lyndon Pryor, guest, *Leadership on the Rocks*, podcast, episode 59, Leadership Purpose and Impact with Lyndon Pryor," February 14, 2024, https://youtu.be/uM1GIhlCw38.

39 Brené Brown, *Braving the Wilderness: The Quest for True Belonging and the Courage to Stand Alone* (Random House, 2017), 147.

40 Kerry Patterson et al., Crucial Accountability: Tools for Resolving Violated Expectations, Broken Commitments, and Bad Behavior (McGraw-Hill Education, 2013).

41 John Maxwell, *Developing the Leaders Around You: How to Help Others Reach Their Full Potential* (Thomas Nelson, Inc., 1995), 9.

www.ingramcontent.com/pod-product-compliance
Lightning Source LLC
LaVergne TN
LVHW010314070526
838199LV00065B/5562